D0040005

BIKE
SNOB
ABROAD

BIKE SNOB ABROAD

STRANGE CUSTOMS, INCREDIBLE *FIETS*, AND THE **QUEST** FOR **CYCLING** **PARADISE**

BIKE SNOB NYC

CHRONICLE BOOKS
SAN FRANCISCO

Dedication

For my wife Sara and my son Elliott, my favorite companions
in traveling and in life.

Text copyright © 2013 by Eben Weiss.
All rights reserved. No part of this book may be reproduced in any
form without written permission from the publisher.

Library of Congress Cataloging-in-Publication Data available.

ISBN: 978-1-4521-0525-3

Manufactured in China

Designed by Suzanne LaGasa
Illustrations by Shannon May
Typeset in Monod Brun and Sentinel

10 9 8 7 6 5 4 3 2 1

Chronicle Books, LLC
680 Second Street
San Francisco, California 94107
www.chroniclebooks.com

CONTENTS

Prologue: **DROPPED FROM THE SKY**   6

Ch. 1: **HANGING IN THERE**   13

Ch. 2: **UNSOLICITED ADVICE**   29

Ch. 3: **"WE GOT A CHILD NOW, EVERYTHING'S CHANGED!"**   37

Ch. 4: **THE ELUSIVE NATURE OF BELONGING**   53

Ch. 5: **BOUNDER OF ADVENTURE**   69

Ch. 6: **SUMMER OF LIKE**   93

Ch. 7: **DREAMS OF ESCAPE**   103

Ch. 8: **IT'S REAL, AND IT'S SPECTACULAR**   115

Ch. 9: **ALL ABOARD THE FLOTILLA OF SMUGNESS**   127

Ch. 10: **SMUGNESS INTERRUPTUS**   145

Ch. 11: **SWEPT AWAY**   157

Ch. 12: **WELCOME BACK**   169

Ch. 13: **ON THE ROAD AGAIN**   181

Acknowledgments   192

Prologue:

DROPPED
FROM
THE SKY

"Where am I?"

This is a game I like to play with myself sometimes. When I find myself in a remarkable situation or setting, I pretend I just woke up and have no idea how I got there. Or, I just imagine I'm that guy from the movie *Memento* who had no short-term memory and basically had to tattoo little Post-It notes all over himself. It's fun—sort of my little way of savoring the moment. And I'm playing it now.

So where am I?

Well, let's see: First of all, I'm piloting a strange contraption. It is, more or less, a bicycle, though there is a great big wooden trough on the front of it with a clear plastic canopy over it. Okay, I must be riding a mobile greenhouse. This makes sense. Bike blogging is not exactly synonymous with job security, so it was only a matter of time before I'd have to rent myself out as a door-to-door gardenia peddler. And there's only one place in the world where you can get a job as a bicycle gardener. So . . .

I'm in Portland, Oregon.

But wait, I can't be in Portland! Last time I was in Portland I felt like I had to pee *all the time*—and I mean all the time—because of all the Stumptown coffee and craft beer. Seriously, I never didn't have to go to the bathroom. I happen to be very fond of Portland, but I also associate certain cities with certain smells, and the smell I associate with Portland is the way your pee smells after you've had a lot of coffee. So since I don't feel like I have to go to the bathroom right now, nor am I actually in the bathroom urinating, then I can't be in Portland.

And yeah, this is definitely not Portland, since even though I'm in a city, and even though it's very damp out, I don't see any mountains in the distance or anybody riding a tall bike while juggling.

Still, that doesn't account for the fact that I'm riding in a city on a huge bike yet nobody's beeping at me. Nor does it explain why there are lots of other people around me on bikes yet none of them are wearing cycling-specific clothing of any kind. It's also definitely the present day, since like half the other cyclists are on cell phones. It's not Critical Mass, or a "Tweed Ride," or a charity ride, or really any kind of theme ride whatsoever. There also aren't any police. This makes no sense—I've never seen this many bikes in one place at the same time without some kind of police presence.

Unless . . .

I'm not in America at all!

Well, it's a good theory, and it would certainly account for the fact a bunch of people are riding bikes at the same time even though it's not a special occasion.

Anyway, it's at this point that I encounter a little hump in the street, and as I crest it I realize that I'm crossing over a pretty funky-looking canal dotted with houseboats. I also notice a sign on the side of a building confirming my suspicion that I'm far from home—it's a street name, and the street I'm on is evidently called something like "Niewenhusenvorbulgraght." Most telling, though, is that I finally peer into the canopy on the front of my rolling greenhouse, and I notice that what I'm transporting isn't greenery at all. It's a young human child who just happens to be my son.

Now I've got it—I'm in Amsterdam.

And this is why I'm playing the game—because I want to savor this experience. Just as countless teens and twentysomethings have sat in Amsterdam coffee houses, stared at each other through clouds of marijuana smoke, and coughed out the words, "I can't *beleeeve* we're smoking *weeed* in like a *baaar*," I can't believe I'm riding what amounts to a station wagon on wheels with my wife Sara just up the street and my son Elliott hanging out in his trough, and I'm being treated like a human being and not a stray dog who's wandered out into the street or an #Occupy[Your City Here] protester about to be washed away with a fire hose.

This treatment is something I didn't even realize I wanted until just a few years ago—mostly because I was almost unable to conceive of it. I don't mean the rolling greenhouse specifically (well, actually it's a *bakfiets*, but we'll come to that) so much as I mean the ability to take to the streets by bicycle free from harassment, fashion, politics, and pretense. See, in America, you ride for fitness, or you ride for thrills, or you ride to make a statement. But as a lifelong cyclist and a new father, I've increasingly begun to realize the pleasure of riding a bike for no other reason than simply getting around. I've dreamed of a place where doing that isn't considered "alternative" and doesn't automatically brand you as an outsider, or at least as "different" somehow. So I packed my family on a plane and we came to Amsterdam, and it turns out that the cycling paradise really does exist.

So now that I know where I am, let's see how I got here.

Chapter 1:

HANGING
IN THERE

One of my favorite things about cycling is that, even though I've been riding bikes for as long as—well, for as long as I've been able to ride bikes, every few years or so it reveals some new dimension to me. It reminds me of a recurring dream I have, wherein I discover some exciting new room or wing in my home that I never realized was there. To me, that's what cycling is like—it's a familiar house I've lived in all my life, but every few years or so I open a door and realize I've got something really cool in there like a Jacuzzi or a 70s-style shag rumpus room.

When I first learned how to ride a bike, the joy and the thrill was simply being able to ride the bike without falling over. I explored and savored the sensations of speed and balance. Soon, though, I realized that the bicycle was also something with the magical power to shrink my neighborhood, and that I could quickly get to my grandparents' house or home in on the distant sound of the Mr. Softee truck. It was also the way I made my first friends, and bicycles were the means by which we undertook our neighborhood adventures.

Bicycles gave us our first brushes with danger and introduced us to the "real world"—the one beyond toys and cartoons and the safety of our households, in which everything was under the control of our parents. Naturally a powerful tool such as a bicycle is highly coveted by nefarious forces, and we quickly learned how to thwart bike thieves. You kept your bike in your sights at all times. You never let a strange kid "try" it. When you saw two older kids on one bike it meant the passenger was about to jump off and give chase to take yours. We were even once ambushed by a unit of bike thieves with stockings on their heads who leaped out from behind the considerable cover afforded by a Gran Torino.

We were chased so often that we learned how to quickly disperse, pigeon-like, at the first sign of danger. Then we'd rally at a favorite spot where we'd breathlessly recount our own individual escapes. Without realizing it we were also mastering our bikes—how to sprint, how to hop curbs, how to ride down stairs, and how to carry our bikes over obstacles. Like the thieves themselves, we were an elite unit, bike whelps that might one day grow up to be the cycling equivalent of Navy SEALs. Our imaginations compelled us to explore our neighborhood, reality compelled us to flee, and our bikes were the vehicles for it all.

If you're an American most of this probably sounds pretty familiar. Most of us grow up with bicycles, and most of us have our formative vehicular experiences and implement our first playful sorties into the real world on them. However, just when our relationship with our bicycles begins to mature we're suddenly expected to leave them. This generally happens around the time we're teenagers, and our teachers and our parents and the older kids start telling us that bicycles are childish, or dangerous, or both. It's when we're expected to start learning how to drive, and preparing for the rite of passage of car ownership. So we break our bond with our bicycles, and more often than not it never recovers.

This very nearly happened to me.

In America, children are expected and even encouraged to ride bicycles, and a large number of adults have always and will always ride bicycles as a form of recreation. However, there are very few places in this country in which a teenager approaching driving age might feel that riding a bicycle as a means of transportation is a reasonable thing to do. Basically, there's no middle ground between that fresh-off-the-training-wheels sidewalk and cul-de-sac style of riding and the "Strap on your helmet and pretend you're a car" approach we adults are expected to practice.

This is certainly true of the place where I grew up. My first bicycle adventures technically took place in New York City, but specifically they took place in an isolated part of the Rockaways called Bayswater that few people outside of the neighborhood even know exists. It's a little peninsula that juts out into Jamaica Bay, and as such there was no through traffic and only light car traffic. In the previous century it had been a place of summer estates, and in many ways it still felt rural. The houses that made up those estates, though decidedly less grand now and in many cases divided into multiple family homes, were still there. My mother would take me on walks and point out what she said were mounds of shells left by the Reck-ouwacky Indians. My friends and I would spend hours exploring the shoreline of Jamaica Bay, with only the landfill across the water and the very distant Manhattan skyline to remind us we weren't the first people to do so. Sure, we were under strict instructions never to actually enter the water lest our flesh melt off our skeletons, but I don't think there was a natural body of water anywhere in the United States that you could safely swim in during the 1970s.

All of this is to say that it was something of an accident of geography that I could ride a bicycle as freely as I did for as long as I did, for it wasn't until adolescence that I began to bump up against the infrastructure that would make riding a bicycle for transportation nearly impossible.

As children, our transportation needs were essentially dictated by the whims of our imaginations. If we needed to go somewhere it was because that was where the ice cream truck was, or because we felt like sitting in that abandoned car at the end of Healy Avenue, or because it was time to jump off our favorite sand dune. In my mind the distances between those various locations seems huge, but when I revisit them now of course I realize that they were only a few blocks away from each other—with the exception of the Mr. Softee truck, which could be anywhere, and which we would probably have chased all the way to New Jersey.

But just as the bicycle rapidly shrinks what was once the immeasurable void beyond your front yard, adolescence shrinks it yet again. This is because adolescents are compelled not by their imaginations but by the popular culture. The sand dune and the abandoned car no longer had any appeal; now it was the twenty-four-hour smoke shop where they had that skateboarding video game, *720°*, or it was the record store where they sold exciting records with covers depicting skulls pulling out their own eyeballs. Most importantly, you do not want to have to rely on those embarrassing middlemen known as "your parents" in order to get around, for to be ferried about by them was the very height of indignity.*

*[Of course I realize nobody actually goes anywhere to play video games or to buy records anymore thanks to all those newfangled "computers" everybody's using now, but I'm pretty sure there are still places adolescents are compelled to go without their parents' involvement. Or maybe there aren't, which I suppose would explain the childhood obesity epidemic.]

By the time I was an adolescent we didn't live in Bayswater anymore—we had moved to nearby Woodmere. Geographically it was similar in that it was also fairly isolated and was only a few miles away from my old neighborhood, but the fundamental difference was that it was in Nassau County and not Queens and it had public schools where the kids didn't pee on your lunchbox. (Yes, at P.S. 104 in Bayswater the kids peed on my lunchbox. I guess either I was one of those kids who had "Pee on my lunchbox" written all over his face, or my classmates just hated *The Dukes of Hazzard*.)

Now that I was getting older and my interests were getting broader and my destinations were getting farther afield, I still relied on my bicycle to get to them. I was discovering another dimension of cycling: that it could take me to school, and to the store, and that I could use it to cover some pretty serious ground. However, at the same time I was beginning to encounter more formidable obstacles to cycling than big kids leaping out from behind Gran Torinos. I was encountering the Gran Torinos themselves, due to the fact that the New York City metropolitan area is of course comprised of Huge Roads with Speeding Cars on Them.

Let's say I wanted to get my hands on a new record that had a particularly grisly skull on the cover. I couldn't just download it onto my iPod because there were no iPods and the Internet was still just a figment of Al Gore's imagination. Instead, I had to go to all the way to Slipped Disc Records on Rockaway Avenue in Valley Stream. So I'd ride the three miles there, chain my bike outside the store with its forbidding smell of leather and vinyl, pay for my grisly skull album with fistfuls of nickels, dimes, and maybe the occasional crumpled dollar bill, and then I'd ride the three miles home again with the record hanging from my handlebars, doing my best not to dog-ear the corners by banging it with my kneecap.

This could have been a pleasant trip, and in many ways it was a pleasant trip, though in other ways it was also kind of miserable. Sure, having honed my SEAL-like bicycle skills as a child I was adept at hopping curbs and darting through alleys and nabbing a little off-road action by skirting the railroad tracks or cutting through the schoolyard or taking advantage of a few poorly secured backyards. However, this was not always possible, and for much of the journey I had to choose between the narrow and uneven sidewalk and the shoulder of a street thundering with motor vehicle traffic heading to and from Green Acres Mall or JFK airport. If you want to feel like you don't belong someplace, just approach Sunrise Highway on a bicycle. It's only marginally less stressful than taking a stroll along a highway median.

In fact, looking back at those days, as I waited to cross Sunrise Highway I was very much at a crossroads. Straddling a bicycle at one of the busiest intersections on Long Island, in pretty much exactly the spot where, back in the late 1800s, a hotel just for cyclists once stood, I was in a place where I didn't belong—at least as far as most people were concerned. Furthermore, I doubly didn't belong because I had a weird imported record hanging from my handlebars and had colored portions of my hair with Lady Clairol.

That I persisted in any of this behavior made me an exception. In retrospect I don't know if I persisted despite being an exception or because I enjoyed being an exception. I do know that by this time pretty much all of my peers had abandoned their bikes, consigning them permanently to the garage or passing them down to a younger sibling. I was the last of a dying breed.

And then my bike got stolen.

So there I was, a teenager who was suddenly bikeless in a country where teenage bikelessness is an acceptable—indeed the preferred—condition as far as "society" is concerned. This was a time during which many things were competing for tiny slivers of my very narrow attention span: records; going to see the bands who made those records; smoking and drinking surreptitiously; painfully awkward formative sexual experiences; and having to go to work for the first time in order to fund it all. Saving up for a new bike that I could use to ply the hostile streets simply fell outside the range of my bandwidth at the time.

So instead, I surrendered to what seemed like the natural progression of things. Going to see bands play and getting trampled by my peers was a deep obsession for me by this point. It had managed to crowd out my previous obsession with BMX racing, at which I now sucked anyway because I had broken my arm and become nervous and squirrely. As for actually getting to these shows, I didn't really need the bike, since I was spending more and more of my time in the city and for that all I needed to do was take the train. However, my need and desire to pilot my own vehicle never died, and so I finally did start saving my money for some new wheels—only those wheels were attached to a car.

This is where cycling ends for most young people—I mean, usually it ends a bit earlier, but for those tenacious teens who are still hanging in there this is the real terminus. The end of the line. The drop-dead date at which point you're supposed to ditch the bike. I'm talking about Driver's License Day.

That might have been it for me, and I might have become a typical noncycling American from that day forward, except for one thing: I love riding bikes. Some of us are just born this way, and our love of riding can exist and indeed thrive in even the most hostile environment. So by the time I got to college my obsession with getting pummeled at hardcore shows began to wane and my dormant love of bikes once again began to stir. Some of my peers had mountain bikes, and road bikes, and eventually I began riding again. By junior and senior year I was taking to the roads of upstate New York on a hybrid bicycle. I wore half-shorts and a fanny pack, and if it was really hot I went shirtless. I often look back at those days and cringe.

Despite my ghastly appearance I was in the process of discovering yet another dimension of cycling. It had carried me through childhood, it had seen me through adolescence, and now it would be my release in adulthood. After college I came back to the city and started my first "real" job, and I continued to ride more and more. I rode laps in Prospect Park before work, and I explored all weekend. I ditched the fanny pack, I got an actual jersey, and I went into debt in order to own a real road bike. My weekend rides got longer. I went to work as a messenger for a while. I started racing. I spent all of my disposable income and most of my non-disposable income on "upgrades." My rides became training rides. I spun fluidly past shirtless people on hybrids and scoffed. Then one day I woke up and realized I was a Roadie.

You know how your parents told you that shaving your hair makes it grow back quicker? Well, that's not true. They only told you that so you wouldn't try to shave your pubes, cut yourself, and then wind up in the ER.

The "shaved hair" theory does apply to people, though, in that when you repress them they come back weirder and more determined. Consider American cyclists. We're encouraged to ride until we're in our teens, at which point we're supposed to stop—and most of us do. However, there's still that tiny percentage who are inclined to do it. These people are strange enough to begin with, but when you put them in an environment that's hostile to them they get even stranger. They wear blinding colors. They spend many thousands of dollars on exotic cycling machines. If they're men, they shave their legs even though everyone around them is horrified and tells them that it's going to make it grow back thicker.

Basically, they become a subculture.

So basically, I had come full-circle. As an adolescent I had been a BMX-riding, hardcore-listening, Lady Clairol-using member of a youth subculture. Now, I was the grown-up equivalent. The only difference was that when I was an adolescent I was still at least able to wear the same clothes both on and off the bike. As a twenty-something I had to don a special outfit and wear shoes that made it impossible to walk, or else the ride didn't count somehow.

Nevertheless, I was a genuine rarity—an adult who still rode a bicycle. I had avoided the anti-bike winnowing process, but only by reveling in equipment and wearing special outfits. But society wasn't done with me, and it wasn't going to stop until I consigned my bike to the basement for good.

As we get older, life has a way of getting . . . life-ier. We take on more responsibility. We start craving actual bed frames between our mattresses and the floor. We launder clothes we once might have left unwashed, and we replace them when they become ragged. Our jobs become more involved and require more of our time and attention. We commit romantically to fellow human beings. These human beings, understandably, want more out of their weekends than spending them alone while you vanish for nine hours at a time on your "epic" bike rides.

While this clump of demands and pressures is not the final obstacle society will hurl before the bicyclist, it is the penultimate one, and the demands of relationship and career have caused many cyclists to unclip for the last time, or at most straddle the old bicycle on the odd sunny day for an hour or two and reminisce about the glory days. As that pack of roadies spins effortlessly by you in the park, you think back on how easily you might once have accelerated and affixed yourself to the back of the pack, and how you would still have had enough wind left to chat with your fellow riders. Then, once you recovered, you'd have taken your turn at the front, or maybe even opened a bit of a gap on the hill just to be playfully competitive.

But now those days are gone, and on the occasion you succumb to that latent urge to jump in, you merely plummet into the gap like

Homer Simpson trying to jump his motorcycle over the Grand Canyon, hocking and wheezing and sobbing over the indignity of it all.

Race fitness is fleeting. More than that, race fitness is addicting, and to maintain it you have to feed it with hours and miles, like a drug habit. Eventually your life demands may force you to kick that habit, and if you try to pick it up again it will mostly just make you sick, like a smoker sucking down a pack of Marlboros after a ten-year hiatus.

Of course, there's a middle ground between abstinence and addiction when it comes to cycling, but because we are all forced off our bicycles by the time we're teenagers very few of us know what that middle ground is:

Getting stuff done by bicycle.

If you use your bicycle to get to work, your career won't force you off your bike. Instead, it will force you onto it. Your relationship also won't force you off your bicycle if you use bicycles to do the things you enjoy doing together. Errands and chores won't keep you from your bike if you use your bike to go grocery shopping. This is because cycling is not the all-or-nothing proposition many (especially Americans) think it is. It's actually extremely malleable—far more so than driving. You can pick up a pretty decent commuting bicycle for the cost of a few tanks of gas, and you'll never, ever have to circle the block for forty-five minutes in order to park it.

Like most Americans, this didn't occur to me immediately, and while I did commute by bicycle it was mostly because I lived in New York where riding a bicycle for transportation has always been, to some degree, a part of the cultural makeup of the city. It wasn't until I got a bit older and less obsessive about bike racing that it occurred to me I could get as much pleasure from errand-running as I could from a five-hour road ride to Nyack. This was something of a breakthrough for me.

Of course, in so doing I encountered a whole new set of obstacles. As a recreational cyclist, I certainly had to deal with a lopsided infrastructure teeming with bad drivers, but perhaps the biggest impediment was the insular nature of bike racing. Like any small group of people, bike racers have their rules and customs and quirks and they can be a judgmental lot. Consequently, you have to undergo a bit of hazing in order to join. Maybe it's sideways glances at your equipment, or people scoffing at your unshaved legs. (In the bike racing scene they laugh at men who *don't* have shaved legs.) It's mostly good-natured, but it also means that to become a recreational bike racer you have to *want* to become one. Not only do you have to acquire a certain level of fitness, but you also have to have the mental fortitude to push through the judgment and not care. But you bring the hazing upon yourself, because you volunteer for it.

On the other hand, the impediments to practical cycling are forced upon you whether you want to deal with them or not. When you're a bike commuter, the hazing comes from the government, and from the media, and even from strangers on the street. Law enforcement either ignores you, or else it treats you as severely for your transgressions as if you were driving a car. (Or often more severely.) Newspapers publish editorials about how ridiculous a form of transportation cycling is, and hundreds of readers chime in to say how they'd love to run you down, or how if you're foolish enough to ride in traffic then you deserve whatever you get. It's easy to buck convention for the sake of recreation, but it's a lot harder when you feel like you're under attack for the simple act of riding to work.

Nevertheless, like a small but increasing number of cyclists, I weathered this too. I parried and dodged and deflected the killer cars and scathing editorials, and I consequently advanced from the American cycling semifinals to the finals.

The final exam, when it comes to staying on your bike, is having a family and riding with them. This is the final frontier. Unless you live someplace like Holland where putting your kids on your bike is about as controversial as letting them watch *Mary Poppins*, if you keep riding a bicycle as transportation with your family, then that's it, you've won. You have taken the KOM points at the top of Mount Smugness. From then on, all the impediments are purely physical and natural: saddle sores, old age, and monster snowfalls are all that are left to slow you down.

But make no mistake—if you live in a motor-centric country the finals are very difficult. Sure, plenty of people continue to race or ride recreationally when they have families—our culture is quite comfortable with middle-aged people who still want to play with expensive toys—but the idea of simply getting around by bike with the family in tow is still profoundly un-American. This isn't to say that hauling kids by bike is unheard of here. On the contrary, it's fairly commonplace, and you'll certainly see people with child seats or trailers in parks and on recreational paths. Like jogging strollers, these devices are sporting goods staples. But once you start setting off into the world with a child on your bike in order to do stuff you'll quickly learn that the typical American views this behavior only slightly more favorably than letting junior play inside the clothes dryer.

This, more than anything else, may be where we get it all inside out, and it's too bad, because it's probably the aspect of cycling from which we have the most to gain.

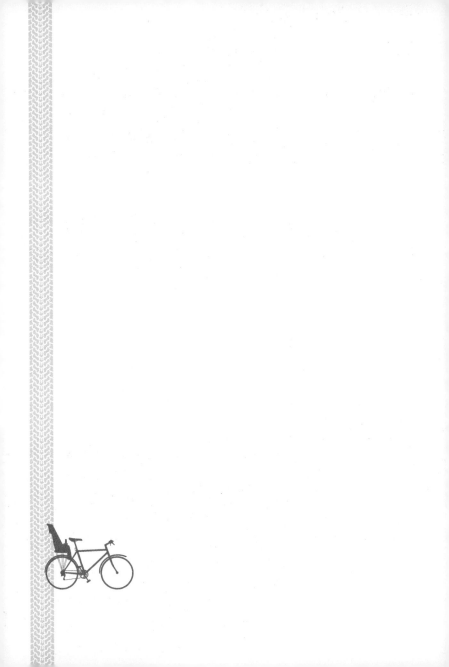

Chapter 2:

UNSOLICITED ADVICE

It's a crisp yet sunny winter afternoon in Brooklyn, and I'm riding along Vanderbilt Avenue on my Surly Big Dummy cargo bike with my year-and-a-half-old son Elliott strapped into the child seat behind me. He is wearing a puffy ski jacket and over his fleece hat is a blue helmet with little cartoon rockets on it. In this ensemble, he looks as though, were I to press some kind of secret button on my handlebars, the seat might eject sending him straight to the moon. He's also perfectly content, as he generally is when he's on the bike.

At a red light, a woman in a Jaguar pulls up next to us and rolls her window down in that manner that almost always prefaces a request for directions, and so I mentally prepare myself. Oddly, while motorists in America have little patience for cyclists, it's clear they also depend on us, because they have no compunction about asking us for directions.

This is because they realize we're more in touch with our surroundings, and so they just assume we know where everything is.

Frankly, I resent the fact that drivers treat us like human signposts. Firstly, I resent it because I resent the slap-and-kiss of alternately being honked at and being asked for directions, and secondly I resent it because I take direction-giving very seriously and so when people ask me how to get someplace I get all nervous like when the teacher used to call on me in school. Knowledge of the streets has long been prized in my family, and by failing to direct a motorist to the nearest Brooklyn-Queens Expressway on-ramp in the most expeditious manner possible I run the risk of bringing shame upon my people. So while asking me for directions may seem like nothing to a misguided motorist, they simply have no idea what they're putting me through emotionally.

Anyway, I'm already visualizing a map of Brooklyn in my mind and trying to anticipate which nearby landmark, establishment, or highway she's in search of when she finally begins to speak and I realize she's not looking for directions at all. Instead, she wants to conduct an impromptu interview with me.

"May I ask you a question?" she inquires with sort of a plastic smile on her face that tells me her "question" is going to be more of a lecture.

Before I can say "No," she continues:

"With all these maniac drivers, aren't you afraid of someone running into you from behind?"

Immediately, various possible responses begin scrolling in my mind, like that scene in *The Terminator* when Arnold Schwarzenegger ultimately goes with "Fuck you, asshole." Actually, at the moment "Fuck you, asshole" is a rather tempting choice, since implicitly criticizing a stranger's parenting choices while simultaneously evoking the specter of bodily harm befalling their child is only slightly more tactful than urinating on their leg. She may think she's merely expressing concern, but the truth is it comes off like a mobster walking into a restaurant while fondling a Zippo and asking, "Aren't you afraid somebody might burn this joint down if you don't pay the protection money?"

But I can't just go with "Fuck you, asshole," since then in addition to being the person who rides heedlessly (as she sees it) around town with his child strapped to his bike, I'm also the antisocial, foul-mouthed scofflaw that she probably expects me to be. As much as I hate to admit it, she's got me exactly where she wants me—either I have to tell her I'm not worried, in which case I'll confirm her suspicions that I'm an awful parent, or else I have to tell her off, in which case I confirm both my awful parenting as well as the fact that I (like everybody who rides a bike) am a lawless jerk.

My only hope is to somehow, in the remaining two seconds before the light turns green, cough up a retort that politely lets her know how foolish and thoughtless she's being. Sadly, this is the best I can do:

"Well, I'm no more afraid than I am when I'm driving him in a car."

This is lame, but true. When I drive my son in the car, I'm acutely aware of all the horrible things that might befall us—just as I am on a bike. I'm under no illusions that my car grants us immunity from drunk drivers running lights at speed, or from being rear-ended by someone who's engrossed in their cell phone, or from being cut off on the expressway by a wannabe racer and dying in flames at 70 mph.

The simple fact is, thanks to cars we're liable to get killed or seriously injured no matter how we choose to transport ourselves, and if anything we should be most afraid in the car. In my home state of New York last year there were 36 cyclist fatalities and about 660 more cyclists were hurt badly enough that their injuries were classified as "serious." Meanwhile, about 1,100 people were killed in motor vehicles, and about 10,500 were seriously injured. Sure, there are more people driving than cycling so it's not surprising more people get hurt that way, but I'm also more likely to get hit by a car while simply pushing my son with a stroller than I am while cycling, since 309 pedestrians were killed by cars last year and about 1,800 more were seriously injured. So, what, we shouldn't walk?

Yet nobody would ever approach me at a light while my son sat in his car seat and ask me if I was afraid, or implicitly question my wisdom or sanity. Automobile travel depends on this blind spot that prevents us from seeing just how dangerous our chosen method of transportation is, and on transferring both our worry and our scorn onto the more "vulnerable" people we see through our windshields.

Unsurprisingly, my reply bounces right off her blind spot and she takes it with a smirk.

"Well," she replies, "He does have all that stuff on him, so I guess he's all right."

The "stuff" she is referring to is the helmet, as well as the ski jacket, which is a bright orange and which maybe she mistakes for some kind of safety suit or flotation device. I'm not sure if she is being sarcastic and trying to insult me, or if she merely thinks a cyclist's job is to bundle himself up in safety equipment and surrender to the inevitable onslaught. It is probably a little of both.

Mercifully, the light finally changes though naturally we catch up with her again at the very next red. She is indicating a right-hand turn, and so I wait behind her to allow her to complete it and to spare myself a "right hook." However, she clearly wants to redeem herself and show me how considerate she is, and so she simply sits there waiting for me to pass.

This is all very sweet, but sometimes when a driver yields their right of way to you it's even more dangerous than when they break the law. At least I expect drivers to speed through that red light just after it's changed, but those awkward standoffs in which a driver yields to you when they shouldn't and everybody behind them starts beeping are fraught with danger. That's when an impatient person floors it from behind them, shoots into the intersection, and runs you over. At best, you become like two people who try to pass each other in a hallway and wind up doing that eternal back-and-forth dance. This is what happens with the woman in the Jaguar. I am determined to let her go, but after a while people behind her were growing impatient, and so I finally went, withholding the wave of thanks she doubtless thinks she deserves.

All of this is fairly typical for a day out on the bike with Junior. I've never actually driven an ice cream truck, but it must be similar to riding a bicycle with a small child on it, because it seems that every time I come to a stop I'm surrounded by people. However, instead of giving me money for delicious treats, they interview me, implicitly pass judgment, and offer unsolicited advice.

Oh, sure, there are plenty of admiring people too—hempy-looking people with beards, mostly, who want to discuss the finer points of bicycle portage, or else people who find the sight of a toddler sleeping on a bicycle impossibly cute and need you to know it—but in my years of riding bikes I've found no type of cycling as polarizing and controversial as family-style cycling.

I've also found no type of cycling quite as rewarding.

Chapter 3:

"WE GOT A CHILD NOW, EVERYTHING'S CHANGED!"

My son was born on March 29, 2010. He was late, so the doctor induced labor, which was convenient since it meant we were able to schedule our hospital visit in advance and I had plenty of time to find us free parking.

This is not a parenting book, so rest assured I'll be sparing you step-by-step diaper changing instructions and my personal feelings on breastfeeding. (Though if you need to know, I think breastfeeding's awesome. It's like nature's soda fountain, right down to the free refills.)

When you're an expecting father, childbirth doesn't actually start feeling real until you're at the hospital and it's all happening. This is true regardless of how involved and excited you are, and I can assure you I was very excited. I coveted children like some people covet Di2 electronic shifting systems or artisanal handmade bicycle frames, and I used to nag my wife constantly for one. Still, the fear and anxiety any reasonable person feels before the arrival of a new permanent roommate didn't hit me until I was about to accept delivery.

Meanwhile, when I expressed this anxiety to my wife Sara as we watched *Along Came Polly* or something similarly vacuous while trying to clear our minds before heading to the hospital, she simply replied," Are you kidding? I've been carrying him for nine months, I just can't wait to get him out."

Well, of course—this was the part I'd never be able to understand. I was about to become a parent, whereas for Sara it had begun three-quarters of a year ago. Sure, I'd gone to the doctor with her and put together some crap from Ikea, but for all practical purposes I was the guy walking into the movie late and getting hushed by everybody else.

And they did hush me, too. The temperature in the delivery room was something like 25 degrees Fahrenheit because when a woman gives birth to another human being she tends to work up a bit of a sweat. I, however, was doing nothing except sitting there trying to look supportive and prattling on about the sociopolitical implications of the film *Along Came Polly* so by about hour ten my lips had turned blue and I couldn't feel my extremities. As I entered the "terminal burrowing" phase that marks the final stages of hypothermia, the doctor walked in and asked, "How is everything?"

"I'm freezing, it's really cold in here," I replied before I realized she hadn't been talking to me, and everyone just turned and stared at me like I was the guy on the *Titanic* complaining about the leak in his cabin.

Eventually, Elliott was born. As humans we tend to live at a bit of a remove from the workings of nature and the universe, but even in the setting of a modern hospital watching your child being born thrusts you face-first into the lawn mower blades of nature in the most shockingly beautiful way. In fact, it was oddly psychedelic in a way that really surprised me, though part of that was probably owing to the sleep deprivation. Nevertheless, delirious or well-rested, it was incredible to think that here was this new person who, as recently as the previous summer, existed only as the potential between two people. Then, there he was, and the moment I first laid eyes on him he looked familiar. "Hey, you're the guy from the sonogram!"

And that was it—we were parents—and we haven't been to sleep since.

Soon, though, it would be my turn to take a pull at the front of the parental paceline. As a person who makes his living by writing sarcastic things about bicycles, I have a certain degree of freedom in my life. Sure, I have to write the sarcastic things, but where I write them, how I write them, and whether or not I wear pants when I do is nobody's business but my own. My wife, on the other hand, does the sort of job where you have to go to a particular building during certain hours of the day, and pantslessness simply isn't an option. This meant that, once her maternity leave ended, weekday tiny human nurturing responsibilities lay largely with me.

This is not some scheme on my part to advance the notion that I was some sort of single parent. As the mother, my wife still did most of the parental heavy lifting (Fun Human Reproduction Factoid #2: Men can't breastfeed), and my own mother was transformed into a grandmotherly superhero by my son's birth and would come over regularly to take care of him. Still, there was always a decent-sized chunk of every weekday during which it was just me and the infant, and without a breast to give him succor I had to do my best to fulfill his needs while simultaneously keeping up a goofy bike blog and writing a book called *The Enlightened Cyclist,* which you should buy not only for yourself but for every single one of your friends. (Also, get three extras for yourself just in case you laugh so hard that you drop the book in the toilet.)

I'm fortunate for many reasons (I'm reasonably healthy, I wasn't born in the Middle Ages, I'm not a barnyard animal, the list goes on) but I count as one of the greatest fortunes in my life the fact that I was able to stay home with my young son while simultaneously working, often without pants. This is not something most employed adults can do (my wife included), and so I felt very privileged. Nevertheless, I did also find myself pining for certain aspects of the workaday world I once took for granted, such as being able to go outside and occasionally wearing shirts that don't have baby doody on them. Therefore, I began to pin all my hopes on a single date: May 29, 2011.

This was because May 29, 2011, would be my son's first birthday, which in turn meant that it would officially be legal in New York City for him to ride as a passenger on my bicycle. Sure, overeager people in Portland had explained to me that I could adapt a car seat to my bicycle so as to carry him even while he still had the useless softball-on-a-bendy-straw infant neck thing going, and I did also talk to somebody who used to carry his baby around in a messenger bag, but I figured I might as well wait until Elliott was able to support both his own head and a helmet like an actual vertebrate. Plus, the spring seemed a perfect time to get him started. While I'm sure you get huge smugness points for cycling with a six-month-old in the winter, that's really not the sort of competition I'm looking to win.

Therefore, I waited for May 29, 2011 as excitedly as I once waited for my own seventeenth birthday so that I could drive a car by myself. Once Elliott was bike-legal, that's when the fun would begin. No longer would we be limited to playgrounds within easy walking distance, where we'd see the same old moms and the same old toddlers. No longer would I have to schlep that stroller up and down the subway stairs like some hybrid of Sisyphus and Michael Keaton in *Mr. Mom*. No longer would we need to use the car for our family outings and then regret it immediately when we wound up sitting in traffic or circling for parking. Instead, we could flit about in Prospect Park like a couple of balls in a pachinko machine. We could visit the zoo at will. We could make the rounds of the neighborhood playgrounds like a couple of barhoppers. We could ride onto the span of the Manhattan Bridge and watch the subway trains go by, just for the hell of it. I could go out and do errands with him, and we could both enjoy it. Surely the mobile phase of parenthood would be my salvation.

In fact, I was so excited that by late April I just said "screw it" and figured I'd give Elliott a head start. The weather was warming up, he was very big for his age anyway, and on the off-chance a police officer stopped us I had a stick-on beard for Elliott as well as a fake ID that said he was twenty-three years old and an ensign in the navy. So I installed a child seat onto my cargo bike and set out for the final frontier of American cycling:

Child Portaging.

I've experienced heightened sensory awareness only a few times in my life. For example, once when I was under the influence of a certain hallucinogen in college, I'm reasonably certain I actually heard the sound of a tree growing. Also, when I was a young child, they used to have these plastic ears at the Bronx Zoo that would let you hear the way a coyote hears. However, these were like being in an alcoholic stupor compared to the heightened awareness I experienced when I first rode a bicycle with my son attached to it. As we set out for a trial run around the neighborhood, my arm hair stood on end to detect any stirrings in the atmosphere caused by approaching motor vehicles. My ears cupped and swiveled like a pair of satellite dishes, and I could hear a cat on a porch two blocks away licking its private parts with its bristly tongue. My eyes migrated to either side of my head, and I could view a 360-degree panorama without so much as moving my neck. Even my tongue got into the act, and it darted in and out of my mouth like a snake's, collecting and analyzing chemical data from the air.

So there I was, riding through Victorian Flatbush like a startled lemur. As for my son, he was as calm and contented as a garden Buddha. (I know this because every so often one of my independently moving googly eyes would wander to the back of my head to check on him.) After a few blocks, his calm state began to calm me, and eventually my pupils contracted, my hair stopped bristling, my ears became flush with my head again, and I began to enjoy myself.

Cycling with my son indeed became a huge pleasure, just as I'd hoped it would. This is true for both of us. From that first ride, the prospect of getting on the bike thrilled him, and riding together soon informed his nascent vocabulary. "Helmy, helmy!" he'd demand as soon as I mentioned the word "bike," and when I gave his helmet to him he'd dutifully plop it onto his head backward. He knew exactly where to find the bike in the parking lot, and I'm reasonably sure that the first time he used the word "yes" it was in response to my asking, "You wanna go on the bike?" Before that, the answer to every question was an emphatic "No."

This wasn't because I was trying to brainwash him, either. Even though I'm a dedicated bike dork, my son is under no obligation to like them. I happily supply him with toy cars, which he happily pushes along the floor while saying, "Beep, beep!" and which he takes an alarming amount of delight in smashing into things. This makes sense, since cars are undeniably attractive playthings to children in the way that bicycles simply are not. A toy car sits there on the coffee table just waiting for you to push it off at high speed, whereas a toy bicycle would just kind of lamely flop over. No toy company is making a "Livable Streets" bicycle and pedestrian advocacy play set, and even if they did I doubt I would buy it.

Yet when it came time to actually get into a car, my son would be distinctly "meh," and then five minutes later he would be soundly asleep. However, when it was time to get on the bike he'd be excited, and while he obviously couldn't articulate it yet, I'm pretty sure this was because he could see everything around him. He could feel the air. He could watch the pavement scrolling away beneath him. He could pull at my underpants and administer a wedgie. You know, the same reasons we all like to ride bikes. (Plus or minus the wedgie part, depending on your proclivitiews.) Really, riding a bicycle was and is so pleasant for both of us, I'm not even ashamed to call it delightful—even though it makes me sound like a commercial for herbal tea.

Yes, it's *delightful*. It elicits within me the sort of happiness one seldom experiences as a city-dwelling adult: pure, sincere, non-ironic, non-spending–induced pleasure. And that's just on the weekdays when I'm in stay-at-home dad mode. When it's the weekends and it's the whole family, my pleasure swells into full-on familial bliss—that is until he drops one of his toys in traffic and we have to stop to pick it up while he cries.

As it happens, I'm also embarking upon my family cycling adventure at a fortuitous time, since New York City is in the process of creating an actual bicycle infrastructure. Like most New Yorkers, I always rode in "survival mode," moving swiftly and obeying (and just as often disregarding) motor vehicle–centric traffic laws as I saw fit. I was fast, and I was aggressive. Then I got older and had a child, and now I am more than happy to embrace the safe, fuddy-duddy, law-abiding cycling style of the baby-portaging parent. It is the bicycle infrastructure that makes this possible, for once-treacherous routes are now family-friendly, and I can undertake many of my journeys in protected bike lanes. Streets where I once dodged trucks and slipped in garbage water now offer me dedicated lanes with plenty of room for my cargo bike, and in these lanes I can pedal in a leisurely fashion while singing the alphabet song and practicing my banana hand-ups (or, more accurately, "hand-backs," since Elliott sits behind me).

Sure, I still like to go fast and kid-less on my bicycle, and when I do I simply head to the open roads upstate or take my mountain bike into the woods where I happily ride into trees. As for practical riding, though, I'm more than happy to mature along with the local infrastructure. I don't mind being domesticated. I want to be coddled by bike lanes. I have no need to be an outlaw. I don't need the simple act of riding to the bagel store to be a nonstop thrill ride. I don't want to jockey for position with cars and trucks. I want only for cycling to be as accessible as possible, and for others to experience the joy of practical cycling that I have discovered, and for it to be so commonplace as to be utterly unremarkable.

But as fortuitous as this time is for family-style cycling, it's also tumultuous in the way that sweeping change can be.

Some time ago, I read an article in the *New Yorker* called "Transformation" by Rhaffi Khatchadourian. It was about recent advances in the area of human face transplants. I'm not talking about having your eyes lifted or your nose done; I'm talking about having your entire face seared off in an electrical mishap and then receiving another one from a dead person, as had happened to the subject of the article. I'm fairly squeamish when it comes to detailed descriptions of surgery so it was difficult for me to read, but at the same time it was so fascinating I was unable to stop.

What was particularly compelling was the psychological implications of face transplants. Of all our organs, obviously it's the face with which we present ourselves to the rest of the world. For this reason, serious facial disfigurement is profoundly psychologically traumatic in a way many other injuries are not. Also, despite what you may see in movies like *Face/Off*, you can't just throw another face on somebody like so much pizza dough. To transplant a face from one person to another is a difficult and extremely risky process, and only now is it becoming remotely possible. When you try to graft a body part from one person to another, the recipient's body often rejects it, and this rejection can be fatal. But for all this difficulty and risk it also has the potential to restore something more than just physical functioning. It can also restore the patient's humanity.

New York City is in the midst of becoming an ostensibly "bike-friendly" city, though the process is not a simple one, and this always makes me think of that story about the face transplants. A century of automobile-centric planning has left the city scarred, and increasingly New Yorkers want more cycling infrastructure to repair the damage. They want riding bicycles to become a part of their lives, and they are demanding—and have begun to receive—amenities like indoor bike parking in office buildings, and miles of protected bike lanes, and traffic lights just for them. Basically, the city's been getting a new face.

At the same time, just as organ transplants don't work like sticking a new pair of eyes in your Mr. Potato Head, building a new bicycle infrastructure in New York City isn't as simple as just grafting it on. In fact, when you transplant an organ, the body's first reaction is often to reject it. There are politicians and civilians who are determined to stop the enhancement of the bicycle infrastructure. In Brooklyn, well-connected residents acting under the guise of "concerned citizens" continue to sue the city to remove bike lanes. In city government, politicians proudly denounce the bike-friendly Department of Transportation while running for office. In the press, cyclists are portrayed as wanton scofflaws and the head of the Department of Transportation, Janet Sadik-Khan, as a "crazy bike lady." One TV news outlet went so far as to suggest that a bike lane near the Israeli consulate would encourage cycling terrorists. Often they're knee-jerk reactions and minority opinions, but nonetheless they remain a real threat to the success of the transplant.

Even some cyclists are resistant to the change, for after all our identity has long been that of resourceful urban warriors who outwit drivers and outrun subways. There's also mistrust, and a notion that if we do get a bunch of bike lanes we'll be forced to ride in them exclusively and will somehow forfeit our rights to the streets.

So we're in a precarious time. As cyclists we've gained a lot, but these gains are tenuous. While the Department of Transportation supports cycling, it also reassures those who question the need for cycling infrastructure that these changes are "experimental." There's a sense that some or all of it could disappear at any time. Worst of all, beneath this infrastructure still exists a basic assumption among many people that, in collisions with motor vehicles, the cyclist is somehow at fault for the simple reason that, even in New York City, riding a bicycle is often seen as a fringe activity. Underneath the new face there's still some seething resentment.

And of course the most dangerous part of resentment is that it can undermine goodwill. The luxurious infrastructure makes me want to respect it and ride more considerately, yet when I read another anti-cycling editorial or another news story about the police refusing to investigate the death of a cyclist, I can't help thinking, "Why bother?" But if we don't bother then we'll all return to the old way of riding a bike in New York City, which is best described as "Every Man for Himself." (And it was mostly men, too, since women tend to be less interested in speeding rodent-like through traffic and racing with taxis.)

So that's where we are now in New York City, and in much of the country. It's a city with a new face, but the surgery is very recent, and there's no guarantee that it will "take." In the meantime, some rides are blissful, and some rides are miserable. Actually, usually a single ride can go from blissful to miserable and then back again in a matter of blocks. Certainly to some extent this is just a part of living in New York, where life is characterized by contrast and dynamism and beauty juxtaposed with ugliness, and where the whole range of human experience is on display.

While living in a neutered New York sort of obviates the reason people live in New York, there are also certain amenities we can and should take for granted without being considered "soft," and these things change over time as we become more refined. At one time it was indoor plumbing. Then it was electricity. Then it was cable television. Then it was the Internet. We got all these things, and New York was still New York.

So now it's the twenty-first century, and we're due for a bicycle infrastructure. Really, it should be as basic and noncontroversial as electricity or Wi-Fi. But the question remains:

How long is it going to take everybody to catch up with it? For the drivers to accept it, and for the riders to use it sensibly? Sometimes I get impatient. Maybe I don't have that kind of time. As "legitimate" as cycling gets, there's still always that sense that you're some sort of pioneer—even though people have been riding bikes for about 150 years now. Maybe I should go someplace where it's already like that. And there are places where it's like that. So what's the point of hanging around here and waiting? I mean, if we didn't have indoor plumbing in New York yet I'd probably just give up and move.

This is when I start flirting with the notion of escape.

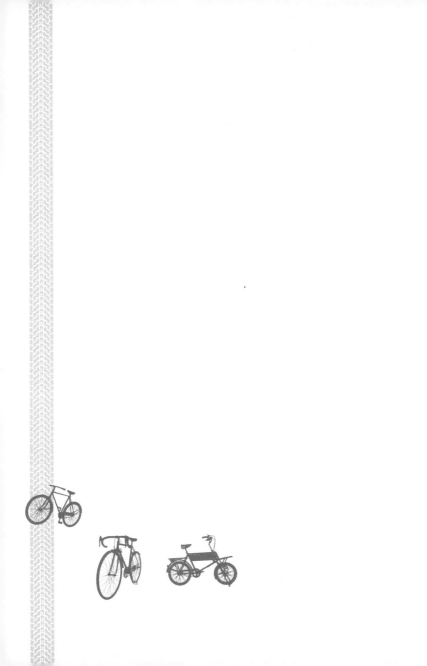

Chapter 4:

THE
ELUSIVE NATURE
OF
BELONGING

"If you could live anywhere, where would it be?"

This is an easy question for some people to answer, and amazingly they just pick up and move. I remember working at my first real adult job at a publishing company in Manhattan. Almost all of my peers had migrated to New York City after college in search of excitement, or change, or some kind of dream. I envied them.

I did not come to New York in search of a dream. I came to New York City because I was deposited in Beth Israel Medical Center, and apart from four years of college in upstate New York I've spent pretty much my entire life inside the same twenty-mile radius. This means my home range is roughly equivalent to that of a coyote. Sure, I have nothing on those people who have spent their entire lives playing dominoes in front of the same walk-up building, but at the same time I could easily visit every place I've lived in a single day by bicycle.

In a lot of ways this is comforting. I love living close to my relatives. I love that my son is growing up here. I love that you can still see the painted sign for my grandfather's business in midtown. I love that I can remember seeing the Twin Towers across Jamaica Bay. I love that when I land at JFK I can see the diner on Rockaway Turnpike where we used to hang out in high school. I love that walking around the Lower East Side reminds me of being a sheltered teenager in search of records and punk shows, self-consciously mingling with the squatters until it was time to catch the Long Island Railroad, and overall I love the reassuring sensation of lifelong familiarity.

On the other hand, I never really *elected* to come here, and like a wandering coyote I often feel shiftless and out of place. Though the city had been a refuge for me as a teenager, I had always just assumed I'd wind up someplace else when I grew up. Granted, I had no idea where, but I always fancied myself as a writer—even when I worked in the local hardware store and looked like some reject from an early incarnation of Soundgarden—and so in the back of my mind I imagined myself ending up in some John Irving–esque New England setting come to life, or wherever Richard Dreyfuss lives in *What About Bob?* Either that, or I'd go to England, which I knew nothing about beyond *The Hitchhiker's Guide to the Galaxy*, *The Young Ones*, and *Monty Python's Flying Circus*, which together formed the entirety of my artistic canon.

But halfway through college I decided I wanted to work in book publishing, and all the book publishing is in New York, and I was able to stay in my old bedroom while I looked for a job and sorted out an apartment. Then I moved to Brooklyn (this was back when you moved to Brooklyn because it was cheaper than Manhattan, and not because there was an artisanal mayonnaise shop on every corner, because there wasn't; in those days it was Hellmann's or nothing) where I commenced my adulthood and where I remain until this day.

Still, I can't help wondering if I belong here, and the reason for this constantly nagging doubt is the bike. The bike is a constant reminder that I am an outsider no matter where I was born. It's a symbol of my lone coyoteness. Even as the city continues to lay mile after mile of new bike lane, and even as the new arrivals embrace the bicycle and continue to transform Brooklyn into something almost absurdly froofy and precious by opening artisanal mayo shops, every *New York Post* article and every Internet cycling death story postmortem comment pile-on reminds me how many people think I'm a freak—just as they did when I was younger and I was ridiculed by my classmates for not liking Bon Jovi, eschewing styling mousse, and for pronouncing the letter *r*.

In fact, as I think of all the places I've ever lived and I ask myself where I was the happiest, the answer is always the same: summer camp. Certainly if I ever experienced anything like Shangri-la, it was those precious few summers I spent in the woods of Maine, surrounded by people from other parts of the country who pronounced their *r*'s and who didn't make gagging noises when you mentioned books and who also hated team sports and Bon Jovi and listened to interesting music like the Sex Pistols and the Smiths. There, we lived in rustic cabins, and we spent our days engaged in outdoor activities or producing art of various kinds.

But how does that help me now? It's not like there's some summer camp for grownups in this country where all people do is engage in crafts in a charmingly rustic setting while riding bicycles.

Or is there?

Well of course there is! It's called Portland, Oregon!

On the surface, it would seem as though Portland would be my ideal city. In practice, though, it's not so simple. I was fortunate enough to spend a week in Portland not too long ago, and here were just some of the many great things the city had going for it:

—Mild (though wet) weather

—An amazing bicycle infrastructure in the city

—Lovely roads for cycling outside of the city

—Good food and drink

—Cyclocross races accessible by light rail

—Lots of bike-themed events

—Lots of bike shops

—Lots of bike companies

—Lots of custom bike builders

—Lots of bikes

—Lots of "bike culture"

—Bikes

On the other hand, there was only one negative:

—By the end of my stay, bikes kinda made me wanna puke.

It's true. I never thought I could get fed up with bikes, but Portland proved me wrong. I certainly didn't want to *ride* any less, but the constant exuberance over bikes was a bit more than I could handle. As I mentioned, I want nothing more than for cycling to be so mainstream that there's nothing at all remarkable about it. I just want the bikes to be *there*, working dutifully in the background while real life happens, like antivirus software or central air conditioning. This is not the case in Portland, where it can seem like every facet of cycling is considered remarkable and is duly celebrated as such. In Portland, they have family theme rides, and "No babies!" theme rides, and high-heeled theme rides, and unicorn theme rides. In Portland, you can take part in multiple naked rides *on the same day*, and doubtless catch a Tina Turner theme ride in between. In Portland, every week a bunch of people take the light rail up to the top of a hill and ride back down it again on little kiddie bikes. This is called "Zoobomb," and amazingly, this passes as a cultural institution instead of a fraternity stunt, and the pile of crappy kiddie bikes they use is considered a city landmark and not a public health risk called Mt. Tetanus.

I love all of this. I love that it exists, and I love visiting, but at the same time I could never live this way permanently. I want to live in a place where cycling is completely normal, yet at the same time phlegmatic enough that the idea of adults riding down hills on kiddie bikes is considered silly, and corroding piles of sixteen-inch-wheeled Walmart bikes are considered unsightly and are carted away like the refuse they are. I couldn't live in Portland for the same reason I could never be a Hasidic Jew. I don't do well in situations where people are reminding each other of their identity every second, and I'd doubtless snap in short order. "Jew this, Jew that, the kosher food, the Yiddish, it's enough already!" I'd scream in *shul* one day as hundreds of severe-looking bearded men turned to glower at me.

I know this would happen because the same thing almost happened to me in Portland. A few days before I left Portland to return to New York I was at yet another bike event and as I looked around the room and saw hand-sewn wool cycling cap after hand-sewn wool cycling cap, and pair after pair of cycling shants, and hundreds of identically tattooed forearms each clutching the obligatory pint of craft ale, I experienced a sudden and intense desire to be somewhere—

anywhere—more diverse. I'd even have settled for my local C-Town supermarket. However, when I closed my eyes, clicked the heels of my Sidis, and then opened my eyes again, I wasn't standing in the produce aisle next to a Bangladeshi woman buying fourteen pounds of a spiny vegetable I've never seen before. Instead, I was still trapped in a wooly bike nerd vegan sausagefest.

And what about the rest of America? What's it like from a cycling perspective? Well, I haven't ridden across country, nor have I even visited all fifty states with a bicycle (or without one for that matter), but based on the places I have ridden I'd say that when it comes to bikes much of the country falls into one of the following categories:

BIKE-XUBERANT

We're all misfits because we ride bikes, and like all misfits we eventually find each other and become the conformists we all despise. In the resultant "Bike-Xuberant" communities, bicycles are basically like recreational drugs in that they make people absurdly happy, inspire them to behave ridiculously, and compel them to wear certain clothes that announce to the world "I love bikes!" Obviously, Portland is the most Bike-Xuberant town in America, but similar behavior is also on display in places like the San Francisco Bay Area. If a city or town has hosted or attempted to host both a Single Speed Cyclocross World Championship and a World Naked Bike Ride, it is probably Bike-Xuberant.

OUTDOORSY

In these locales, people who may or may not have retired early from lucrative banking careers live their lives inside quasi-rustic luxury homes set against stunning mountain backdrops, own top-of-the-line sporting goods, drive Subarus, and engage in seasonally appropriate outdoor activities such as (depending on the climate) skiing, hiking, rock climbing, boating, surfing, and yes, cycling. You won't find these people stuffing bills in the g-strings of racers at a single-speed world championship, and you probably won't find them riding to the store either, but you will find them climbing mountain passes on $15,000 carbon fiber superbikes and training for ultra-endurance races in other outdoorsy locales. Outdoorsy locales include Colorado and Hawaii.

I RIDE A BIKE BECAUSE I SUCK AT GOLF

Remember that banker we just met? Well, now picture his or her uncoordinated counterpart who lives in a somewhat less stunning part of the country. In search of an impact-free outdoor pastime that requires expensive equipment yet doesn't require them to be able to hit a tiny ball into a hole three miles away, this banker then buys a $6,000 carbon fiber time-trial bike, has the shop install about 400 centimeters of headset spacers to replicate the fit of a Rivendell, and then rides it around the local subdevelopment in a sleeveless vest, half-shorts, compression socks, and sneakers. This approach to cycling is commonly on display in warmer, flatter areas such as South Florida.

URBAN

Once a city reaches a certain size (think New York, Chicago, and Los Angeles) it is more or less impossible for cycling to eclipse all other facets of the culture there, as it has in Portland, Oregon. At the same time, it is large enough that most forms of cycling exist there. In the same way that an infinite universe is statistically bound to contain life somewhere other than Earth, a city of a few million people is likely to contain roadies, and mountain bikers, and impossibly smug bakfiets captains, and people who collect recycling on old found ten-speeds, and all the rest of it. Nevertheless, due to the lack of Bike-Xuberance (which cannot exist when the population at large does not smile upon and celebrate cyclists for doing something "special"), none of these groups will so much as talk to each other.

While our major cities have recently begun to take steps towards making cycling ordinary by adding bike lanes so that the rest of the world will not laugh at how impossibly backward they are, this is still America (where many people actually believe free parking is a constitutional right), so there is always a vocal component of the populace that hates the bike lanes and is convinced they're a terrorist plot designed to rob them of their liberty.

BIKES? YOU MEAN THOSE THINGS AT WALMART?

As amazing as it may seem, there are places where bicycles are in fact completely noncontroversial and ordinary. However, they're not ordinary in the "Sure, I ride my bike for transportation every day, what's the big deal?" way. Rather, they're ordinary in the "Bikes? Yeah, you'll find those in the toy department next to the battery-powered Hummers for kids" way. The nice thing about places like this is that the bikes are cheap and accessible, but the bad part is that they also tend to be sluggish mountain bikes assembled by people in vests who do things like install the forks backwards and leave the V-brakes unhooked so it's less of a V and more of an underscore. It's the transportation equivalent of eating Cheetos for lunch.

"THEM"

"Them" is not a place. Rather, "Them" refers those who ride a bicycle because they have to—maybe because they deliver food for a living, or because they live in a transit-starved area and can't afford a car. While you'd think that a group of people who actually ride for necessity would be at the vanguard of ordinary cycling, the unfortunate fact is that instead, the rest of the cycling world alternately ignores or reviles them. The "bike culture" ignores them because they don't wear the right shants or the right hat. "Serious" cyclists hate them because they ride erratically on their delivery bikes. The activists don't advocate for them, since they don't speak the language of policy and advocacy. Nobody embraces them, and nobody is moving quickly to put bike lanes under their wheels. Sometimes it can seem as though bike infrastructure goes where it's wanted, not where it's needed. If you ever find yourself in an unfamiliar American city looking for a luxury condo development or a restaurant that serves locally grown food, just follow a bike lane and you're sure to wind up there. However, if you want to find the neighborhood where the guy who delivers food by bicycle for that restaurant actually rides his bike home, just follow the trucks, and if the potholes keep getting worse you'll know you're headed in the right direction.

THE EXCEPTIONS

I realize I've portrayed cycling America rather bleakly, and that there are exceptions everywhere. There are neighborhoods, towns, and cities where cycling is an unmitigated joy—just as there are neighborhoods and towns that don't allow cycling at all, like Black Hawk, Colorado, where they actually banned it. As for the hospitable places,

Madison, Wisconsin, is as pleasant a place as I've ever ridden a bicycle. Miles of separated bike paths; signs just for cyclists; students and regular people riding bikes just to get places. I was even denied an interview with the local NPR affiliate because I told the host I wanted to talk about acrimony between drivers and cyclists, and she actually said, "We don't have that here."

SO DO WE HAVE AN UNDERLYING NATIONAL CHARACTER?

Like so much in America, cycling varies from city to city and state to state. This is because we are a vast country—so vast that we have two detached states, one floating around in the Pacific and another one nuzzling the tail end of Russia. We've got tropical, and we've got tundra. (For now, anyway. Remember that gasoline commercial "Drive your engine clean?" Well, it seems we may be driving our planet free from ice caps.) We're so big you could fit nineteen Spains in us. We're so huge that we have we have six time zones (or seven if you count Arizona where they refuse to observe Daylight Savings), and we're so disparate in our thoughts, feelings, opinions, and mores that every state has different laws about stuff like guns, marijuana, abortion, how old you have to be before you can drive, and whether or not you can legally hire a prostitute.

Moreover, each region in this country has a history that is profoundly different from every other region. Granted, I wasn't a very good student so I'm fairly hazy on that history, but I think I've got the basics. The story of New England is the Pilgrims coming, being saved with turkeys by the Indians, repaying them with smallpox, and then unwittingly eating fermented grain stores, totally wigging out, and starting the Salem witch trials. The story of Manhattan is the Dutch buying the island from the Indians for some random crap, then the

English taking it from the Dutch, then people who work on Wall Street taking it for themselves, and now nobody else being able to afford anything on it. The story of the Wild West is people coming from the East in covered wagons in search of land and fortune, warring with the Indians, and now we have weird places like Utah. And so forth. Really, the only thing America has in common from a historical perspective is never failing to stick it to the Indians.

Still, despite all these differences, we do have a unifying national character. We cherish our freedom and independence. Thanks to our Puritan forebears and their proto-LSD freakout, we're extremely tolerant of even the most bizarre religious beliefs (provided, of course, they don't involve anybody called Muhammed or Allah). We love our fast food, and even though we account for only 5 percent of the Earth's population we collectively weigh as much as the remaining 95 percent.

But in a country this vast, is there a single place where you can go to see, feel, smell, and experience the American national character? Yes, there is. There's a little mini America that's been baking in that national oven we call the desert that has turned into a harder, more intense version of its full-size counterpart. This little mini America is called Las Vegas.

Las Vegas happens to be the home of Interbike, which is the American bicycle retail industry's big annual convention, held every September. But I was not there for Interbike, as I am not a bicycle retailer. I was actually there a week before Interbike, for my brother's bachelor party. Here are the first things I noticed upon arriving in Las Vegas:

—Every aging popular American entertainer of any consequence has brought their live act here for embalming.

—Should you need a break from drinking and gambling, there are also people who are more than happy to take your money in exchange for letting you spend an hour firing machine guns at inanimate objects.

—They have a fake, sanitized New York City, as well as lots of other fake, sanitized versions of various landmarks from around the world.

—My hotel had a fake beach where you could pretend it's still possible to frolic in an ocean free of oil spills and used prophylactics.

—Nobody rides a bicycle.

Actually, I shouldn't say nobody rides a bicycle, since plenty of people ride bicycles recreationally in the Las Vegas area. However, nobody rides a bicycle *in the city*. I know this because I tried it myself. The morning after my arrival I naïvely put my bike together and figured I'd go explore the town a little bit, and I don't think I've ever been more uncomfortable on a bike—at least not on one with a saddle still attached to the seatpost. Riding in Las Vegas was marginally less horrifying than riding on an expressway. I'm a staunch opponent of sidewalk riding, and as a New York City cyclist I've always been as comfortable as it's possible to be in traffic, but in Las Vegas every self-preservation instinct I have told me the sidewalk was where I should be. Anyway, it's not like there were any pedestrians using them.

So I gave up on exploring the city by bike and instead retreated to my hotel. Even without the bike, I still felt out of place. The slot machines, the fake beach, the indoor restaurants, the indoor rock club complete with artificially distressed interior—all of these things made me feel vaguely queasy, like I was watching a pair of first cousins making out.

This is not to say I didn't have a wonderful time with my brother, because I most certainly did. We rented Harley-Davidsons (Americans are slightly more tolerant of bikes when they have big flatulent motors and five-figure price tags) and took a beautiful ride out into the desert. Then, when we got back into town, it was about 150 degrees, and because the red lights are like seventeen minutes long in Las Vegas the giant air-cooled V-twin engine very nearly melted my crotch into something with the asexual smoothness of a Ken doll's genitals.

But it was worth it for the brotherly love and the desert views.

Still, I just couldn't shake that sensation of nonbelonging. Here I was in Las Vegas, the place celebrated in movies like *The Hangover*; the rock in America's crack pipe; the place upon which people of every stripe converge to forget their troubles and lose themselves in revelry. Yet there I was skulking through the halls with my head down just as I had in high school, and snarling about the irony that Las Vegas is home to America's biggest bike show, and that companies flog high-end commuter bicycles in a town where practical cycling consists of riding Walmart bikes on the sidewalk in order to distribute flyers for strip clubs.

So what's wrong with me? Why can't I embrace the air conditioning, and the convenience, and the cars, and the salesmanship, and the Motor-Vehicular Industrial Complex? Why do I suspect that our national character, whether it's cycling or anything else, essentially consists of a profound and unstoppable willingness to Buy Shit?

Maybe I've always felt this way because maybe I don't belong in America. Maybe no cyclist does. Maybe the same chromosomes that make us like riding bicycles for transportation make us dislike things like slot machines, all-you-can-eat buffets, cover bands, and all the rest of it. Maybe we belong someplace else.

But where?

chapter 5:

BOUNDER
OF
ADVENTURE

I love to travel, even though I'm not very good at it.

When I was young, the country I most wanted to visit was England. The truth is, I used to be kind of an anglophile—not one of those smart anglophiles who knows lots of stuff about Queen Victoria or spends his spare time trying to work out who really wrote Shakespeare's plays, but rather a lowbrow anglophile who was infatuated with British popular culture. (Or at least with the very small amount of British popular culture I had access to in those dark pre-Internet days, which probably bore little resemblance to the actual popular culture an actual British person would have experienced.)

For example, as I mentioned earlier, I loved TV shows like *Monty Python's Flying Circus* and *The Young Ones*. Like any young American comedy nerd I could recite entire episodes, and also like any young American comedy nerd I was completely oblivious to what in retrospect was the obvious disgust of the people who were forced to listen to me.

Naturally, it follows that I also loved *The Hitchhiker's Guide to the Galaxy*, as I previously mentioned, and for the most part that comprised my knowledge of English literature—that and *Pride and Prejudice*, which they made me read in school, but which didn't exactly resonate with me to the same degree, Mr. Darcy's aloof charm notwithstanding.

But England wasn't just a place of great television and literature, for there was also the music. Nobody did squalid, gurgling music quite like the English, and I combed the city for nearly identical albums from nearly identical bands that made music that sounded like it had been recorded in nearly identical condemned houses. As a freshman in high school I knew someone who had just returned from squatting in England. He had an air of adventure about him that was enhanced by his smell, and he returned not only with a formidable head of dreadlocks but also with what must have been one of the first Napalm Death recordings to hit these shores. This was before Napalm Death became a metal band, and when I heard it I felt exactly like Navin Johnson in *The Jerk* when he hears the white people music. "This is the kind of music that tells me to go out there and be somebody!" I thought as I listened to what sounded like a man regurgitating into a toilet bowl in a bathroom with poor acoustics. Of course going out there and being somebody basically just meant sticking another piece of metal in my ear or transferring more album art to my pants with a Sharpie, but it was all I really had to work with at the time.

This was what I thought England was—a zany madcap land filled with absurdist comedy and punishing music. Whereas at home I felt alienated for my strange clothing and my affinity for Britcoms, I knew that England would be a land teeming with silly walkers, college students of every subculture, welcoming squatters, and grindcore bands, and that if I visited I'd surely be asked to either join a squat or join a comedy troupe in short order. Maybe I'd even get to stage a radio play on the BBC.

Then I finally went there on my obligatory postcollegiate trip to Europe and found that it wasn't really like that.

Even though by the time I was out of college my obsession with Monty Python and cacophonous music had waned, I was nevertheless a little disappointed to find that London was less like a Terry Gilliam cartoon and more like a big, busy city that felt not unlike New York. I also discovered I'm not a very good traveler, since when I'm uprooted I tend to get homesick and depressed. Plus I don't like moving from place to place, I like to be comfortable and have regular access to a private restroom, I get nervous when confronted with unfamiliar turnstiles, the whole do-you-tip-or-not thing fills me with anxiety, and I'm virtually incapable of befriending new people.

But as I got older and traveled more I learned that much of the pleasure of travel is the way it confounds your expectations—those tantalizing hours sitting on a plane wondering what the place you're visiting will be like, and then emerging in a jet-lagged haze and seeing if you were right about any of it. Usually the things that strike you first about a new country are the things that never occurred to you, like the way the place smells. Certainly my primary motivation for traveling is not to savor new and exotic olfactory experiences, nor do

I walk about sniffing the air like a beagle trying to lock in on a scent, but nevertheless it is something I notice.

In any case, once I learned this important truth about traveling—that places give you what they have, not what you want them to give you—I began to enjoy it more. In fact, I began to crave it. A trip abroad became like an LSD trip—something filled with infinite possibilities and the promise of escape. When you're in another country, the surprises you find in the ordinary are disorienting yet addicting. I remember visiting Japan and standing in a supermarket aisle that, at first glance, looked like any I'd ever been in, but when I looked closer I realized that most of the food items seemed to be dried tentacles. It was like that moment when you take your first hallucinogen and say to your friend, "I don't think it's working," and then just as you do, the walls start to bulge and the dirty socks in your laundry hamper start writhing like snakes. That's just how I felt in the supermarket— between the jet lag and the unfamiliar smells (yes, Japan has a smell) and the illegible-to-me alphabet and the strange foodstuffs, it was just enough to trigger a psychedelic experience and make me feel as though the supermarket was going to ensnare me in its tentacles and eat me.

But no matter how exhausting your trip is, and how relieved you are to get home, you always end up doing it again sooner or later, and nobody who enjoys travel passes up an opportunity to undertake a voyage. And that's why I went to Gothenburg, Sweden.

I've denied any belief in such a thing as a "bike culture," though to be honest, in doing so I've been a bit disingenuous. The truth is, in any society in which the bicycle has been marginalized or subjugated, two people with an affinity for cycling can trust each other quite a bit more than two random schmucks with absolutely nothing in common. In fact, you could share a religion with someone—an entire moral code of divine provenance that tells you not to kill them or steal their crap or covet your neighbor's wife—yet misunderstandings still arise, and people still take advantage. You can't ask a stranger to watch your bike for you just because you're both Christian, or Jewish, or Zoroastrian. It's just not enough. Sure, maybe if you're both Hasidic or Amish or something like that it could be enough to go on, but that's only because there's so few of you you're bound to bump into each other again at the minyan or the barn-raising and the embarrassment is just not worth the risk.

If you're both cyclists, though, this reduces the risk exponentially. Of course it doesn't eliminate it altogether, and of course it also doesn't mean we're morally superior (we're probably able to trust each other for the same reason the Amish can—you don't want to steal someone's bike if you're liable to wind up at the same charity ride), but the fact is that cyclists tend to look out for other cyclists.

This is why when the Nigerian prince emails me I ignore it, but when some guy I'd never heard of named Hans Stoops emailed me to ask if I wanted to come to Gothenburg, Sweden, for a bike festival I simply said "Yes" and replied with my passport number so he could arrange a plane ticket.

Here are some facts about Gothenburg, Sweden:

—It is in Sweden.

—It is the second-largest city in Sweden.

—It is the largest seaport in the Nordic countries.

—It is the home city of Volvo.

—It is the home city of the melodic death metal genre.

I knew none of these things when Hans emailed me, and I still didn't know them when I accepted his invitation—not even the thing about the death metal. See, there was no such thing as "melodic death metal" when I was involved in that sort of music. Death metal wasn't *supposed* to be melodic, and to my increasingly hairy old-man ears the very term "melodic death metal" sounds absurdly oxymoronic, like "silent rapping" or "chipper goth." In fact, I didn't know any of those things until a few days before I actually got on the plane and decided to run Gothenburg, Sweden, through the ol' Wikipedia.

The other thing I didn't know was what the purpose of this bike festival was. All I knew for sure was that it was called the Göteborgs Cykelfestival, and that the club behind it and of which Hans was part was the Komet Club Rouleur. Oh, and also this:

Den 11 juni fyller vi Lagerhuset med cykelkultur. Filmer, föreläsningar, utställningar, cykelturer, loppis, fest och tävlingar—vi hoppas att Göteborgs cykelfestival kommer att bli en årligt återkommande mötesplats för alla oss som har cyklar och cykling som passion.

I don't know what any of that means.

Having never been to Sweden or to any place in Scandinavia, naturally I also left with my own set of preconceived notions. These were equally if not more banal than my English assumptions, and were based on the only three Swedish things with which I had any firsthand experience: Ingmar Bergman, Saab automobiles, and of course Ikea. I had discovered the films of Ingmar Bergman in college, where I used to watch them in the library in a carrel desk on giant laser discs the size of pizza pies, and I loved them very much—the actual despair of Bergman's films made the cartoonish despair of the music I was listening to seem so fatuous and amateurish that I pretty much stopped listening to it. As for Saabs, I owned a used one briefly, and that too filled me with a sublimely Bergmanesque despair due to its frequent mechanical problems. And Ikea of course is universal and ubiquitous—the Swedish equivalent of McDonald's—and chances are you're reading this on an Ektorp sofa at this very moment.

This was all I knew going in.

On a Friday in early June I finally arrived in Gothenburg, having endured a three-hour delay before takeoff from Newark due to thunderstorms and then a missed connection in Stockholm, where the airport did look and feel in its architecture not unlike an Ikea—though unlike an Ikea it was quiet and easy to navigate. My connection in Stockholm was also the first time since 2001 that I hadn't been made to remove my shoes before going through security, which was a nice surprise. It had become a reflex for me to start getting undressed as soon as I saw a conveyor belt, so when they stopped me and actually treated me with dignity I almost felt like I was getting away with something. I never dreamed that walking through a metal detector with my shoes on could feel so liberating.

By the time I arrived in Gothenburg the delays and lack of sleep had laid waste to my psyche, and fortunately Hans was kind enough to meet me at the airport. I had just assumed he was Swedish, even though in our emails his English had been better than mine, since lots of people from countries like Sweden speak better English than Americans do. In fact, while browsing the bookstore in Newark airport, one of the employees had stepped out from behind the counter and asked, "Do anybody needs any help?" Sure, I don't necessarily expect the bookstore in Newark airport to be staffed by MFA candidates, but the juxtaposition between that and the Jonathan Franzen novel that I was contemplating buying at that moment was jarring nonetheless.

(This is not to say that I'm an intellectual. In fact, I skipped the Franzen because it looked long and scary and instead decided to go with Rob Lowe's autobiography.)

In any case, as it turned out, Hans's English was excellent not because he was Swedish but because he was actually an American from Washington state who had been living in Sweden for quite a number of years. As a New Yorker, lots of the people around me are foreign-born, and naturally I take it for granted that they came here for the freedom, opportunity, better standard of living, abundant fast food chains, first crack to see franchise movies in the theaters, and so forth. In fact, I don't even bother to ask them why they've come, since I've been conditioned to believe that most other countries are impoverished, oppressive hellholes. So when I meet an American who has moved abroad more or less permanently I'm always intrigued. "Wow, you actually left!" I think to myself. America is the big-budget tentpole shoot-'em-up feature at the multiplex that is the world, and it takes a certain amount of gumption to walk out.

As we made our way into the city I asked Hans what the cycling was like in Gothenburg—not the recreational cycling, but the practical, everyday cycling. He replied as if I'd asked him how the pasta was at the Olive Garden. According to him, like most cities Gothenburg had been taking steps to enhance its cycling infrastructure, but it still left a lot to be desired. As he explained this, I looked out the window of his car and saw people riding city bikes on a protected path, and I also saw no yellow taxis or car services running lights and otherwise molesting pedestrians in crosswalks. Sure, this was unsurprising—Gothenburg is a fraction of the size of New York City—but I also noticed the absence of something else you find in any American city no matter how small: the menacing SUV, its windows blackened, throbbing ominously with hip-hop.

The Roving SUV Emitting Throbbing Music (RSUVETM) is such a fixture of the American roadway that we've become used to them, but when you're away from them for a while you realize how outsized and awful they are—they're straight out of some dystopian science fiction future. If I'd been transported in time from the 1950s I'd probably think they were part of some paramilitary *junta* whose purpose was to spread consumerist propaganda and terror. I'd also love to know if there was a pre-motor-vehicular analog to the RSUVETM in the late nineteenth century. Did people ride around on wagons as raucous jug bands played on them? Is this behavior the product of life in a conspicuously consuming automotive culture, or is it something in the American DNA?

Anyway, despite Hans's dismissal regarding the state of practical cycling in Gothenburg, at first glance it actually looked kinda nice. This was further bolstered by the uncluttered, mostly attractive but occasionally prosaic appearance of this harborside city with its mix of low-slung old and modern buildings and its stevedoring cranes which reminded me of Red Hook, Brooklyn. Sure, some of the new buildings were utilitarian enough to be ugly, but the juxtaposition between them and the older, more attractive buildings made the city seem informal and approachable—the sort of city that had dark and moist corners in which subcultures could probably take root. I could also sense the forest nearby—or at least I thought I could, since on the drive from the airport there were signs for moose crossings. It felt less like the blonde-wood-and-

Bergman Sweden I had imagined and more like a city in the Pacific Northwest.

We stopped by Hans's building, where he lent me an old Bridgestone mountain bike that had been converted into a single-speed, and then he installed me in my temporarily vacant host apartment in a tidy modern building where I would be sharing the tidy spare bedroom with the owner's bicycles which hung from a wooden rack on the wall above the futon.

Hans's club was holding a *Big Lebowski*–themed alleycat that night (this may or may not have had something to do with actor Peter Stormare being from Gothenburg, I don't recall exactly), but even if I had not been profoundly tired I cannot imagine that I'd have participated. Instead, I watched the sun set over the harbor from the terrace, which at this latitude didn't happen until about 11:00 p.m., and I savored the opportunity to watch the city slow down and eventually come to a halt in broad daylight. It was beautiful yet oddly melancholy, though that was partly due to my exhaustion and my distance from my family, which always makes me sad. Then I read some of the Rob Lowe book, and soon I was asleep beneath some stranger's Coppi road bike.

As I slept, the sun dipped briefly below the horizon and then came back up again almost immediately, and by the time I awoke it had been up for hours like a grandmother who's very excited about your visit and has been making breakfast for you since 3:00 a.m. So I struck out on my loaner Bridgestone for the Götaplatsen, where the local "bike culture" was set to rendezvous for a ride over to the festival. On the way I reveled in what to my eyes seemed a very European combination of protected bike lanes, cobbled side streets, light motor vehicle traffic consisting of compact cars, and ordinary-looking people doing fairly un-American things like walking together on a sunny Saturday morning or riding their bicycles while carrying their children on them. I also passed a sizeable procession that included a couple of gentlemen wearing top hats and pushing a small keg of beer in a baby stroller. This, I learned later from a commenter on my blog, was the "enlightened members of Porter Drinkers Association on their annual excursion to the city of Kungälv." (Thank you, person named Peter.)

By the time I arrived at the Götaplatsen, a decent-sized plaza bounded by the city's cultural institutions and presided over by a naked statue of Poseidon, the Gothenburg "bike culture" was assembled and fluffing its plumage. At first glance, all of its components were familiar to me: the fixed-gear riders trackstanding laconically, the families with cargo bikes, the wool-jersey-clad retrogrouches with their classic frames, the tall-bike rider, and even the requisite guy wearing tweed and riding a penny-farthing. A woman proceeded to address the crowd in Swedish with the aid of a microphone, and we soon rolled out and headed for the venue.

As we rode, I marveled in particular at the track bike riders, some of whom were wearing messenger bags and riding bicycles I would categorize as "High Tarck"—meaning they featured extensive color coordination, overly narrow bars, and of course a complete absence of brakes. Here was a style that, for the most part, had its origins in my theft-ridden, gridlocked hometown, and had evolved during a time in which crime was rampant and the idea of amenities for cyclists was as absurd as the notion of a graffiti-free subway. You could squeeze a bike with narrow bars between two buses while fighting your way through Times Square at rush hour; you could easily lock it from a street sign or in a stairwell; there was little on it for the thief to pilfer while it sat there. One thought nothing of such a bike, since the point of such a bike was that it was unremarkable—the city had essentially just winnowed it down to something resembling desert scrub. It was a featureless feature of the landscape. That was just what happened to bikes after they'd lived in New York awhile. They became clipped and businesslike, just like their owners.

We all know what happened next, and as the city got safer, recent arrivals saw these unremarkable bikes and found their unremark-ability remarkable. At the same time the city got safer and cleaner in general, and of course the bike lanes started appearing. Eventually, people started building high-end versions of this desert scrub, and more companies rushed to supply them with colorful parts. Riders locked these bikes in front of new bars instead of in old stairwells. Soon this style spread to the rest of the country, and then to the world, and now here I was seeing it in Gothenburg, a place that appeared to be blissfully free from most of the misery that had caused these bicycles to evolve in the first place. This isn't to say I felt contempt for these riders; quite the contrary. In a way, as a New Yorker, I found the homage flattering. At the same time, though, I did find it amus-ing, just as I did when I first heard French rap.

The festival venue was in a place called the Lagerhuset, which is a former industrial area on the waterfront that has recently been gussied up by the city and given over to more culturally progressive uses such as the holding of bike festivals—the sort of "urban renewal" we're familiar with in New York and in most American cities, and which I suppose is also echoed in the whole "urban cycling" phe-nomenon. Outside the space a trials rider was hopping onto stacks of shipping pallets like a pouncing cat, and inside there was plenty of exposed brick and an array of bicycle exotica comprised of everything from racing recumbents to antique track bikes to custom handbuilt road, mountain, and cyclocross bikes of the sort over which bike dorks love to slaver. There was also a room in which films were being shown, as well as a stage from which people were giving presentations to the crowd, and from which I would be giving the last presentation of the day.

As for the presentation itself, in planning my visit I had of course asked Hans what he would like me to discuss. So he talked with the festival organization, and the consensus was that "It seems people are most interested in hearing your thoughts on the phenomenon of your status as a blogger, and the potential this medium has for communication and social change, in the context of cycling."

"Holy crap!" I thought, "Smart crowd."

Frankly, I figured I was in trouble, since any time I've spoken in America people mostly just seemed happy with stuff like pictures of hipsters riding fixies with their asscracks exposed. These bilingual and well-educated Gothenburgers were surely going to make Swedish meatballs out of me and my lame buttcrack jokes.

International travel does have a way of making you think more, though—even if you're someone like me who considers Rob Lowe literature and who's so lowbrow your eyebrows are on your big toes. So by the time I arrived at the venue I'd actually really started thinking about cycling and the Internet as more than just a delivery vehicle for exposed asscrack photos. In fact, here I was at a bike festival in Gothenburg for the simple reason that I had started a smartass bike blog, something I never could have done in the pre-Internet days. Sure I could have been a pamphleteer like Thomas Paine or broadcast my bike-themed musings via ham radio, but I doubt it would have had the same appeal. Moreover, on the way to the festival, I'd followed a rider on a fixed-gear bicycle with purple rims and a white chain that the Internet had almost certainly inspired him to build. And then, as I browsed the bikes on display at the festival itself, I started admiring some particularly nice mountain bikes with the name "Johnsen" on the downtube. Before long, I was talking to the builder, a guy named Truls Erik Johnsen from Norway, and as efficiently as he had built his eponymous bicycles, in the course of the conversation he also gave structure to my thoughts.

In America we're currently enjoying what the cycling world likes to call a "handmade bicycle renaissance." Traditionally, building racing bicycles by hand was the province of European craftsmen, but now there are probably more custom frame-builders on a single Portland block than there ever were in all of Europe, a phenomenon I call the "custom inversion." Meanwhile, builders like Truls are in turn being inspired by this American-led renaissance and resurrecting the craft in Europe. It's not easy for him, though. In America the proliferation of builders also means the proliferation of other craftspeople the builders need, like people who paint bicycle frames. In Portland it's probably easier to find someone to paint your frame than it is to cut your hair. In Norway, however, there's essentially nobody to paint your bike, which means either shipping the frame a long way to get painted, or else turning it over to the guy who cuts your hair and hoping for the best.

Of course, this cultural transatlantic feedback loop is nothing new; it's been happening since colonial times, and arguably the whole custom bike inversion phenomenon sort of mirrors what happened with rock music in the 1960s. But what's different now is the speed and fluidity with which it happens, thanks to that creepy hive mind called the Internet. It's like that whole Edward Lorenz chaos theory "Does the Flap of a Butterfly's Wings in Brazil Set Off a Tornado in Texas?" thing, except now it's more like "Does some American Internet custom lug porn inspire someone in Berlin to start building bikes?"

With the Gothenburg fixed-gear riders still fresh in my mind (mostly because they were still hanging around outside trackstanding), Truls pointed out to me that today certain youth subcultures are being born entirely on the Internet. Consequently, their members look and act the same, regardless of geography. This may be obvious to you if you were born after Kurt Cobain's suicide, but to people like Truls and me who were interested in the punk subculture in our youths and had to subject ourselves to all manner of indignity in order to find it, it's totally fascinating how much things have changed. I wouldn't have had to ride my BMX to Valley Stream or take the train into Manhattan to find those Amebix records. I wouldn't have had to physically obtain a paper copy of the *Village Voice*, ask someone in the record store or some guys loitering on a stoop, or listen to the hardcore show on the NYU radio station in order to find out where and when a certain band was playing. I wouldn't have had to wait for my friend to return from overseas with that very first Napalm Death record in order to hear grindcore for the first time. In retrospect, we were like Charles Dickens fans used to be, waiting by the dock for the new chapbooks from England so they could find out what happened to Nell in *The Old Curiosity Shop*. Now, the sharing is instant and requires no direct physical contact, and so prospective members of a subculture all get turned on instantaneously regardless of geography, like a great big string of Christmas lights.

This was what was happening with cycling. Sure, I realized it on a certain level while following the track bike riders and musing about how disassociated the style looked in Gothenburg, but until Truls articulated it for me I hadn't really contemplated or appreciated the swift and frictionless quality of the process. I'm judgmental and bewildered by it in an old-person knee-jerk kind of way, but when you really think about it, it's kind of beautiful—passion working on the same circuit all over the world.

Our conversation cut through my jet lag just in time for me to take the stage and give my presentation—the final one of the day and the first one in English—and the festivalgoers were kind enough to indulge me even though I later found out I had sweat rings under my armpits the size of pie plates.

With my duties as a bike festival presenter now out of the way, I was free to enjoy all the cultural stimulation that Gothenburg had to offer. I felt light and unburdened in a medium-sized city of earnest Swedes. The city was, as they say, my oyster. Unfortunately, I also had to board a plane in roughly thirty hours, so I'd have to shuck that oyster and slurp it down quickly.

That night the Komet Club Rouleur hosted a post-festival party at a nearby bar. I found my way to it by following a gentleman with a Rip Van Winkle beard and a Pedersen bicycle, which is a bike of Swedish design that looks like the illegitimate offspring of a penny farthing and a hammock, and between his vaguely Dumbledorian appearance and the striking engineering of his two-wheeled contraption I felt as though I was being shepherded into some sort of alternate cycling dimension. In fact, in a way I was, for when I arrived I found that the entire bar had been given over to a bike-dorkian bacchanal. Inside there was roller racing, and outside Hans, Truls, and I settled at a sidewalk table and talked more about "the world" in that way people do when they're from different countries—where we were from, where we had traveled, and the ways our respective homes had changed during our lifetimes. We were in a neighborhood of older buildings, and for the first time during my visit I saw a bit of motor-vehicular ostentation in the form of a passing Maserati.

It was a Saturday night, and as we sat and conversed in the small window of time during which the Swedish summer sun actually has its head below water, I thought once again about interconnectedness. There was no Internet now, just three people brought together by cycling and talking about their lives, and here I was thinking about mine while looking at the streets of Gothenburg and learning about Truls's homeland—the small, petroleum-rich nation of Norway—in such a way that I felt like I was transcending time and space and inhabiting three places at once. It was like looking at three over-laid transparencies that resolve themselves into an entirely new landscape.

This is the most intoxicating quality of travel and the one that, for all its speed and accessibility, even the Internet can't replicate. The Internet will allow you to memorize international facts or binge on another country's popular culture by proxy, but there's no substitute for sitting over a beer with a blond Norwegian whose features speak of his Viking DNA and a culture thousands of years old as he tells you about his country, or of hearing the story of a fellow American who had moved to Sweden and begun a family there, and who could move between my culture and the one we were currently in with ease. It's something that makes you feel connected to the place you come from, and to the place you're visiting, and to humanity in general, since as long as people have traveled they've almost certainly sat around eating and drinking and sharing their lives—except when they were killing each other in the throes of xenophobia, of course, but fortunately none of us were inclined to force the other to worship our respective gods, or to bludgeon the other for having a different opinion on the respective merits of various bicycle frame materials.

Most of all, though, experiencing this old-fashioned interconnectedness is tremendously reassuring. When you're sedentary it's easy to fall into something like solipsism, and to view the people and events of the world at large as incidental plot points in your own personal narrative. It's also easy to feel alone—like the American cyclist, for example, forced into the gutter and spat upon by an automobile-centric culture. Travel reminds you of the folly of solipsism, and of the fact that your reality is not necessarily *reality*.

The next day was Sunday and my last full day in Gothenburg before my return flight early on Monday. As it happened, the bearded gentleman who had guided me to the afterparty was the proprietor of a small bike shop around the corner from where I was staying, and he was kind enough to invite me to join him and the rest of the Komet Club Rouleur riders for an early morning coffee.

It turns out that partaking in coffee with people (called *fika*, which is *not* a Swedish pop group) is a deeply important part of Swedish culture, and so we sat on the sidewalk in the morning sun that had been up for like fourteen hours already and fika-ed away. In a detail that further endeared the Gothenburg cycling community to me, I learned that the bike shop owner was in fact a bus driver who maintained the shop in his spare time out of a love of cycling—quite a difference from the stereotype of the ornery bike shop proprietor. He also made a mean fika. This wasn't just the kind of coffee that puts hair on your chest; rather, it was the kind of coffee that burns the hair off your chest and then instantly causes you to regenerate a completely new pelt. This, I should emphasize, is a compliment, and the coffee was just what I needed to rivet my jet lag and the weird solar patterns into something resembling circadian alignment.

As we talked, people came and went: Truls en route back to Norway with his family, various members of the bike club, the Czech recumbent builders, and as they did I began to understand the appeal of the fika and the casual interaction it fostered. In particular, I got to tell hard-luck stories. One of the best things about being an American in a country like Sweden is that, even though you're from one of the wealthiest and most powerful nations in the world, you actually get to complain. See, in America (and most of the world for that matter) as a person with a roof over my head, a TV full of bad cable programming, and a snack drawer full of Doritos, I'm nothing more than a bloated lump of privilege. In a place like Sweden, however, I've got the "street cred" of a war refugee. Just watch a Swede's face as you tell him or her about our lack of free health and dental care, and our paltry six-week maternity leaves, and our stratospherically expensive higher education system that has people mired in student loans until they're grandparents. You'll score pity points by the fistful at your next fika.

The only problem with this is that it works both ways, and when they tell you about their subsidized daycare, lengthy maternity and paternity leaves, sick days for both children and parents, and free higher education you may become jealous enough to throw hot fika in their faces. If this happens, simply do your best to rationalize your rage away by thinking about their higher taxes and six hours of daylight in winter. It probably won't work, but at least it will help.

Post-fika, Hans, another frame-builder who built bikes under the name of Godspeed, and I went for an off-road ride on the pine-needle-carpeted trails in the lushly ferny forest of one of Gothenburg's many parks. This was the equivalent of being able to vanish into the woods of Central Park, and as someone who loves to ride on dirt this was certainly one of the most decadent urban cycling experiences I'd ever had.

The next morning, Hans took me to the airport, and I left both profoundly exhausted and brimming with goodwill towards this cycling community that had embraced a complete stranger, listened to his sarcastic musings, suffered his sweaty armpits, and fêted him with fika. The feeling was still with me when I landed in Newark on one of those perfect cloudless May days, and I thought maybe that I had brought the goodwill back with me and it had manifested itself in meteorological form.

Maybe, I thought to myself on the cab ride home, all I needed was a change of scenery. Maybe my "I'm an outsider and everybody hates me because I ride a bike" feelings were merely paranoia. Maybe things would be different from now on and I'd ride the streets basking in the sunshine of human goodwill. As I thought these things I attempted to tune out the driver's angry cell phone conversation, which contained frequent use of words like *maricón* and *hijo de puta*. Occasionally, another driver would do something he didn't like, and so he'd move the phone aside and direct the same invectives towards the offending motor vehicle instead.

Soon I was home, and as I was leaving the cab the driver attempted to overcharge me. I refused to pay the extra amount. He went silent for a moment, and then he fixed my eyes with his and pointed one index finger towards the beautiful blue cloudless sky that had offered me such hope just a few moments before.

"You will die very soon," he intoned menacingly. "Mark my words. You will die very soon." Then he drove off.

I was officially home.

Chapter 6:

SUMMER
OF
LIKE

Despite the fact that I had been cursed by an evil cab driver and was liable to die at any moment, the summer was indeed mostly a pleasant one, and the fair weather always has a way of lulling me into a false sense of security and making me think, "Hey, maybe things aren't so bad here in New York after all."

The truth is there's a lot to do on a bicycle in New York City, and try as they might the overzealous police and the anti-cycling politicians and the homicidal motorists just can't ruin it, because you simply can't stop people from doing something this practical and fun. Bike races abound if that's your thing, and all sorts of other riding opportunities are available if you're actually a sensible person and prefer to leave that sort of thing to the Lycra-clad Warriors of Delusion. Put on your best half-shorts and join a charity ride! Round up some friends and go to the park! Saddle up with your loved one and dine alfresco at one of Brooklyn's many charming restaurants! Or just ride over the bridges and enjoy the view of the greatest city in the world while dodging wobbly tourists on rental bikes! Do I sound like some sort of tourism board commercial? Do you get the impression my smile has been forcibly plastered to my face? That's because it has been, and this veneer of delight is all that's keeping me sane!

But really, there are a lot worse places to be (Las Vegas, for example, or New Delhi in India, where a young boy once wiped what I'm pretty sure was feces on my arm for a laugh) and traveling around New York City by bicycle in fair weather during the long days of summer is often a real pleasure—until it starts getting *really* hot, at which point riding a bike starts feeling like someone has poured a lukewarm cup of tea down your pants.

On May 29, shortly before my trip to Gothenburg, we celebrated my son's first birthday by loading him and about 150 pounds of picnicking supplies on my cargo bike and heading to Prospect Park, where we threw a little birthday party. There was some falling down and some crying which was inevitably followed by some passing out, but that's typical of me when boxed wine is involved. Elliott on the other hand was a perfect gentleman. This birthday also marked his officially being bike-legal, though as I mentioned we'd been flouting that for at least a few weeks by then.

At the party, both my parents separately expressed their concern over our means of travel in the way grandparents are obligated to do. (This despite the fact my mother used to ride me around Bayswater, Far Rockaway, on her British racing green Raleigh three-speed.) However, I remained comfortable with our choice. Had we driven to the park we would have spent more time circling for parking than actually traveling, thanks to all the other people doing the same. Plus, if you've never been to New York you'll be either fascinated or horrified to learn that people here like to park their cars as close to the park as possible so they can leave their car doors open and their stereos blasting while they picnic at the park's edge. This is because many people here live in mortal fear of holding conversations in normal tones, and they grow extremely nervous if there's not something for them to shout over at all times. In any case, this "PA system" approach to picnicking is not only depressing, but it also means these spots are particularly coveted and thus parking can be very difficult to come by.

After my return from Gothenburg my wife and I continued to revel in the joys of familial cycling. We also discovered (or in my case rediscovered) that underrated and overpolluted local natural resource known as "the beach," and as it turns out the Timeless Call of the Sea may end up becoming a vital factor in a New York City cycling renaissance.

When I was a young kid in Far Rockaway, we used to spend a lot of time on Atlantic Beach, where my grandparents had a cabana. If you've seen *The Flamingo Kid* then you have some idea of the New York beach club milieu. If not, imagine the sound of the waves mingling with the braying voices of mothers with large hair ordering hot dogs and hamburgers from cabana boys, and the sight of aging men from the garment district with sun-purpled skin and gold *chai* medallions nestled in their chest hair playing cards, and the pitter-patter of children's feet running up and down the wood-slatted alleys between the cabanas and the lockers. It was a very happy place for me, and to this day I find the smell of suntanning oil to be a source of great comfort, although I stop well short of slathering it on myself before going to sleep.

As I got older, though, I drifted away from the beach, in part because it did not suit my misfit persona. I developed an aversion to shorts and insisted on wearing jeans and combat boots all year round, which is good for skulking around the East Village but far from ideal for sand and surf. Moreover, the beach also represented my peers by whom I did not feel accepted and who all seemed to land the choice beach gigs in the summer like valet parking dentists' Mercedes and fetching sandwiches for those braying mothers due to their high standing in the community. (My brother managed to land one of these jobs. I went to work in the hardware store, where I was alternately abused by a deranged boss and the various plumbers and contractors who would grow impatient with me due to my lack of expertise in PVC fittings and threaded fasteners.) Most of all, there was the time at the beach I fell asleep without sunblock. When I woke up two hours later my chest was a deep aubergine and the source of great pain, and over the course of the next few days it bubbled like a pizza pie which eventually fell off my chest in a single horrific piece of charred flesh. This was all the confirmation I needed that I should remain a pallid landlubber who combed record bins in the city beneath the sickly glow of fluorescent lighting, and that, for many years, was that.

For years I avoided the beach, but as I got older and began riding a lot I would find myself going from Brooklyn to Rockaway. The old bungalows and rambling wooden houses of that peninsula compose some of my earliest memories, and the first place I explored by bicycle was the shore of Jamaica Bay. So on summer days, propelled by nostalgia, I'd ride through the part of the Gateway National

Recreational Area that spans the bay, and I'd see nary another cyclist on those lonely, reed-lined bike lanes. It was a good thing too, since in those days I'd still likely be wearing the whole half-shorts-and-fanny-pack ensemble.

As I aged and conformed and became more "serious" about cycling (by which I mean I joined the racing clubs and did the group rides and rode the races and generally wrung the fun out of the whole enterprise like an Amish woman washing her husband's overalls), I would still slip off every now and again for a bicycle nostalgia tour of the Rockaways. Really, the only time you'd see cyclists out that way in any significant numbers was on Tuesday nights, when they had bike races at Floyd Bennett Field.

Suddenly, though, at around the time Elliott was born, I started noticing other cyclists on other days. Not the people on department store bikes walking their dogs, or the aberrant guy wearing sneakers and riding a carbon time-trial bike, or the neighborhood couples on beach cruisers, or even the occasional roadies who would sometimes pass through to scope out the Floyd course. No, I started seeing the young and the "cool"—exactly the people who had been taking over the East River bridges and the newly-installed bike lanes of Brooklyn and Manhattan. Now, here they were on their track bikes retrofitted with upright bars, wearing oversized plastic glasses, toting messenger bags full of beach towels, and generally exposing their pale and newly tattooed flesh to the hot Rockaway sun.

Suddenly, my words were colliding in a stunningly George Costanza–esque fashion. Here, deep in a territory which not only symbolized my youth but which I had also taken for granted as deeply and profoundly uncool were the very denizens of trendiness. This was my timeless refuge, and now it had been "discovered." Was there no escape?

At the same time, though, it was also heartening. Here, after all, was a beautiful stretch of beachfront just a few miles from the most densely urban portions of Brooklyn—and with a bike lane network, no less. Why shouldn't more people discover it? More importantly, it was a sign that people in New York were starting to think differently. Not too long ago this place had been "too far away" for these kinds of people, since you had to take a long subway ride or a car. However, once you factor in the bike it's not "too far away" at all. Really, it's a perfect destination.

In the late nineteenth century when the bicycle was first invented, cyclists would often ride from Manhattan to what was then the resort area of Rockaway. The resort days were long gone, but now people were finally doing it again.

With a young son my nostalgia peaked—I remembered how much I had loved the beach as a child. I started craving the sand, salty air, and laziness, and so we started taking Elliott to Rockaway, though I resolved to slather myself with sunblock so as not to bake any more pizzas on my chest. To my amazement there were hundreds of bikes locked up all around the boardwalk. It was as though a great wave had washed over Williamsburg and then deposited the entire neighborhood right on the beach.

A wise man once wrote, "Everything about riding a bicycle compels you towards beauty," and that man was me in my book *Bike Snob*. It is true, though, and the Rockaway renaissance is a perfect example. Once you embrace a form of mobility that eliminates traffic and reliance on public transportation the city becomes a lot more accessible and there's a lot less resistance between you and the park, or the beach, or some far-flung neighborhood. When you depend on the car, though, you end up planning your life around avoiding traffic and finding parking. Everything about a bicycle does indeed compel you towards beauty, but everything about a car just compels you towards places with parking lots.

And even though my reflexively contrary nature makes me look sideways at some of the nü-beachgoers, it's not hard to see how much the city could change as people adopt the bicycle not only for commuting but also for recreation—not Lycra-clad, competitive recreation, but let's-go-to-the-beach recreation, or let's load a bunch of crap on the cargo bike and have a family picnic. It's heartening that the appeal of nature still has the power to influence our way of life even in a city this big, and if it's possible here maybe there's still hope.

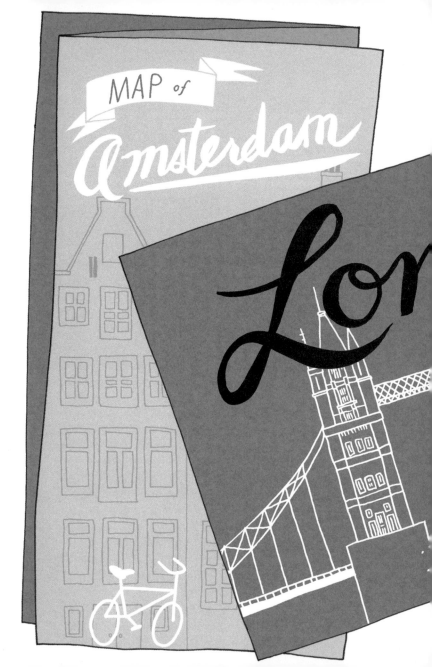

MAP of **Amsterdam**

Lon

Chapter 7:

DREAMS
OF
ESCAPE

Dreams of a brighter tomorrow in which it's normal for regular people and families to ride bicycles are all quite lovely, but for now it's still mostly young Brooklynites riding to the beach to show off their latest tattoo acquisition.

What good is that to me now?

Riding bicycles with my family is one of my greatest joys and one of my most treasured conveniences, yet too many people still look at me when I do it like I'm Michael Jackson dangling his kid off of that hotel balcony. I also know that, should some misfortune befall me while I'm on my bicycle, regardless of the true circumstances, I will bear some or all of the blame. Internet commenters will say that I was "probably running the light," or that I somehow got what was coming to me from the drunk driver going the wrong way down a one-way street in a 5,500-pound Denali because I wasn't wearing a helmet, or that I didn't have "adequate respect for the power of the car."

Of all these common ways in which we like to blame the victim, it's that last one—failing to respect the power of the car—that's in many ways the most upsetting. Really? Is failing to respect a car the problem? Or is the problem that they don't have enough respect for the value of human life and expect others to yield to their consumer goods? Have we really become so skewed and twisted that the *people* are supposed to respect the *cars*? Have we surrendered our humanity to consumerism, and our streets to our appliances? Is America the fabled land of freedom and opportunity, or it is it a land in which you have no claim to public places unless you own the right stuff? Is America the ultimate melting pot—just so long as all that molten humanity is forged into SUVs? In fact, in this country, owning or leasing a car is almost a prerequisite for humanity. You're not a person unless you're paying hundreds of dollars a month on a loan or a lease. Isn't this a form of indentured servitude?

Even in New York City with its vast public transportation network and its swarms of pedestrians I'm constantly reminded of this. New York City is different from the rest of America in many ways, but not when it comes to valuing cars over people. Statistically, according to a recent study, I live in the third-most dangerous neighborhood in New York when it comes to getting hit by cars. If I want to cross the four-lane avenue to go to the store I only have the "walk" sign for seven seconds, and even then I still have to dodge all the speeding drivers who fail to make the yellow. Hundreds of cyclists and pedestrians were killed by cars in 2011 in New York City, yet almost none of the drivers were charged with any wrongdoing—and that includes the ones who didn't even have licenses.

In the past, if you had asked me to choose a cycling dream vacation, I would have come up with something like a tour of the Alps, or a chance to ride the cobblestones of Paris-Roubaix, or some kind of "epic" mountain bike trip in the Pacific Northwest. Now, what I wanted was to experience what it's like to ride a bicycle with my family completely free from oppression. And that's how we wound up in Amsterdam.

Actually, we didn't just wind up in Amsterdam. First, we went to London. Then we went to Amsterdam.

To really understand a person, it always helps to meet his or her parents. Would you marry someone without first meeting Mom and Dad? Not only does this provide additional insight into who a person is, but it also affords you a glimpse of what a person might possibly become. If you're going to enter into a lifelong commitment to another human being, you should at least get a sense of which parts are going to start sagging, which areas are going to start protruding, what pattern the inevitable hair loss will take, and which areas are going to compensate for that hair loss by sprouting gray tufts.

If I was going to stay in New York, shouldn't I meet its parents to get some idea where this place was headed? And who are New York's parents, anyway? Well, I think it's reasonable to say that New York's parents are Amsterdam and London. I don't know which is the mommy and which is the daddy, or if it's a my-two-mommies or my-two-daddies scenario, but London and Amsterdam are certainly our cultural forebears. Sure, we all know that the *real* parents of New York City were the various native tribes who lived here, but the evils of colonialism is a subject beyond the purview of this book, and in any case we can all probably agree that Amsterdam and London are responsible for turning New York into the glorious hellhole that it is today.

In 1614, the Dutch started a settlement on the tip of Manhattan, and this settlement was called "New Amsterdam." Peter Minuit famously paid sixty guilders for Manhattan island, and while there's some argument as to how much that is in today's money, it's probably about what you'd pay now for a nice dinner and a night at the theater. The Dutch also settled the surrounding areas that would eventually become a part of modern-day New York City. By 1664 the Dutch had surrendered New Amsterdam to the British, but to this day you can see Dutch DNA all over the place, particularly in the form of all the Dutch street and place names: Amsterdam Avenue, tons of stuff named "Stuyvesant," Midwood (*Midwout*), Flatbush (*Vlacke bos*), Brooklyn (*Breukelen*), and so forth.

After the British took over, New York City became a major trading port, and we all know what happened from there—lots of bickering that ultimately resulted in everybody's favorite revolution. Incidentally, after the rebels took a beating from the British in the Battle of Long Island, New York remained under British control and served as their base until the war ended and it became, for a time, the capital of the United States of America. In 1790, New York City became the largest city in the country, a position previously held by Philadelphia, which then went on to invent the cheesesteak.

And that brings us to today. Now, New York City, the love child of two mighty world powers, is one of the most important cities in the world. As hardscrabble as life has been here over the centuries, it's also a child of privilege. And while its Dutch place names evoke parent #1, its considerable size and its position as a modern-day economic and cultural powerhouse (not to mention its ostensible primary language of English) call to mind parent #2. Just smoosh Amsterdam and London together, add about nine thousand Ray's Pizzas, and you've got New York City, right?

So while my main goal was to schlep my family across the Atlantic so we could experience the mythical hassle-free cycling of Amsterdam, the city widely touted as the most bicycle-friendly in the world, I also figured we should check in on the other parent to see what cycling looked like there as well. That way we'd get the full picture of our own home city's childhood.

On an evening in early September, Sara, Elliott, and I boarded a plane at JFK, and early the next morning we arrived at Heathrow, where we took the train into London. We were bedraggled, though we were able to make our way to the Waterloo apartment a person by the name of Jack Thurston was kind enough to lend us while he was on his honeymoon. Here are the first cycling-related things I noticed on the way to our temporary home:

1) Outside of Waterloo Station there was actually bicycle parking—not just a rack or two like they have in America, but a whole bicycle parking lot. I should not have found this remarkable, but I did, because I come from a place where "bike parking" means "chain your bike to a signpost until the landlord or the police cut it off." This is not an exaggeration—when President Obama visited New York in 2010 the police removed all the bikes parked along his motorcade route and hauled them off in trucks. The explanation was that it was a "security measure," though if they thought the bikes contained bombs I'm not sure why they felt safe enough to stand next to them as they sawed through the locks, and then just threw them onto flatbed

trucks. Couldn't they just have a bomb-sniffing dog take a whiff of them instead?

2) British cyclists are way into the Day-Glo vests.

3) They have a bike-share program!

This last observation was the most compelling one to me. As I write this (it helps if you picture me sitting at a Victorian rolltop desk with a pad of construction paper and a big box of Crayolas), New York City is preparing to install a bike-share program as well. If you're unfamiliar with the concept, basically it consists of a bunch of automated kiosks all over town. These kiosks are stocked with bikes, and when you want one you just swipe your credit card and take it. Then, when you're done, you drop it at another kiosk. If you're wondering what keeps people from simply making off with the bikes, there are two primary deterrents: 1) They have your credit card and will charge you a fortune, and 2) The bikes are ugly and weigh about three tons, and nobody in their right mind would want one.

Presumably by the time you read this New York's bike-share program will be operational, and either it will be a smashing success or the dawn of a new era of unprecedented carnage. In any case, I'd never tried the whole bike-share thing, but I'd heard the program had been working well in places like Paris, Montreal, Minneapolis, and even Washington, DC, and so I was curious to sample it myself.

There was only one problem: you can't really ride one of those bike-share clunkers with a fourteen-month-old. I mean, presumably you could jury-rig some sort of child seat that you could carry around with you and then affix to the bike when you needed it, but that sort of MacGyvering was well beyond what I was prepared to do during the course of what basically amounted to a two-day stay.

So instead we went to Shoreditch, a now-fashionable neighborhood that had once been rough and indeed was the hunting ground of Jack the Ripper, and I got measured for a bespoke cycling coat.

I should point out that, on my own, I would never get a bespoke cycling coat since I generally find most of the items in my regular noncycling wardrobe to be suitable for around-town riding, and if I'm going to be spending the day engaged in the pursuit of recreational cycling I'll wear full-blown cycling clothes. Sure, those cycling clothes are no good off the bike, but if I'm spending the whole day riding I don't really want to be off the bike anyway. I'm fine being clipped in and Lycra-ed, and once I'm on the bike I'm committed: it's like a cruise, or an LSD trip.

Nevertheless, a storied British saddle company called Brooks had partnered with a tailor by the name of Timothy Everest to make traditionally-styled "technical outerwear," and they wanted me to try one of their jackets. So we traveled to the Georgian house in which Mr. Everest works, and as I stood on those centuries-old wood floors surrounded by antique furniture and racks of jackets for bankers and advertising executives and who knows who else, and as I eyed the very expensive jeans placed next to period-correct windowpanes and subtly lit by the feeble English sun, I was measured for a garment by Mr. Everest himself. As he worked, a restless and jet-lagged Elliott did his very best to destroy the place.

These were considerably different environs than those in which I had been measured for my last bespoke suit. That garment was a rental tuxedo for my high school prom (I opted for the jacket with the tails, naturally), and the environs in which I had been fitted for it was behind a storefront in Lynbrook across the street from a high-end men's *coiffeur* establishment with the evocative name of "15 Barbers No Waiting." Certainly this experience was a bit more atmospheric, but I couldn't help feeling as though making a fine garment and then putting me in it was a bit like hand-painting an elegant bone china soup bowl and then using it to serve Cap'n Crunch.

In any case, I mention this not to give you more insight into my wardrobe than you could possibly want, but because it underscores something which is coming to characterize twenty-first-century urban cycling: the "Fancy Pants Phenomenon."

In the last few years, the increase in cycling-as-transportation has inspired companies both new and old to design high-end clothing that allows you to ride comfortably while looking "normal." The pitch for these clothes is generally along the lines of "These pants are just as at home on the bike as they are in the boardroom," and the image might feature someone on a vintage racing bike juxtaposed with this same person in a trendy loft office wowing a potential client with his ad campaign pitch.

The Fancy Pants Phenomenon is a good thing, since it's a sign that cycling as transportation has entered the mainstream at least to the extent that a company like Levi's now feels compelled to make clothing for it. Moreover, some of these garments are truly excellent. At the same time, though, it also speaks to this complex relationship we have with our bicycles, and our inability to simply jump on them and ride them without first donning special clothing—even if that special clothing is cunningly designed to look like regular clothing.

The Fancy Pants Phenomenon is also yet another reminder that we're living in the age of constant refinement—also a good thing, but nevertheless an amusing one. Supermarkets offer a bewildering array of beers that would have made Archie Bunker's head explode. Middle school kids are ordering espressos and opining about coffee blends. Our musical genres have become as esoteric and hyphenated as our baby names. If the universe tends towards chaos, then the consumer tends towards fickleness, for every year we're offered subtler and subtler gradations of product differences over which to deliberate— hence the perceived need to completely reengineer our wardrobes in order to sit on top of a bicycle for twenty minutes a day.

So as one of Everest's employees showed and explained to me what they were doing, I began to sense that the Fancy Pants Phenomenon was truly an international one, and I also began to wonder if maybe I was witnessing a crucial mutation in the DNA of Western clothing. As more and more people ride, maybe there will come a day when all clothing accounts for this—longer sleeves, reflective piping, more flexible and water-repellent fabrics, higher waists in the back of the pants to ensure that the gluteal cleft stays beneath the horizon. It's all a little precious, but it's certainly more heartening to think about than the fact that some jeans manufacturers are actually recalibrating their waistband sizes (calling a 36 waist a 34, for example) so we don't all start realizing we're becoming obese.

Thusly measured, the next day we bid a temporary farewell to London (I'd be back soon enough) and the next day departed for Amsterdam.

Chapter 8:

IT'S REAL
AND IT'S
SPECTACULAR

Amsterdam Centraal train station is surrounded by bikes. Not a demure little Brazilian wax of bikes, but a vast, dense, lush thatch of the things. They're in front, and in back, and on either side, and even floating on barges in the IJ, which is the brownish body of water that separates Amsterdam from Amsterdam-Noord. The magnificent explosion of bike parking at Amsterdam Centraal made the bike parking at Waterloo Station look like a single sad ingrown hair, and I immediately felt embarrassed for having been impressed by it.

This was it, the official start of our search for what it feels like to ride bikes as a family in a place where it's completely normal.

Upon detraining, Sara, Elliott, and I made our way to the rear of the station to wait for Dries. Dries was the guy from the real estate company that had rented us our apartment, and as we waited for him we scrutinized the various passers-by and tried to guess which one might be him. At a certain point a man scanned the crowd as though he was looking for someone and then walked away. I decided this must be Dries, and so I entered spy mode and set off in search of him. I lost him in the crowd, and when I returned to Sara and Elliott the real Dries was already there with them, which made me feel like Jason Bourne's slow-witted cousin.

Dries was, unsurprisingly, on a bike, and once we were all assembled we joined a bunch of other people (also on bikes) and boarded a ferry across the IJ to Amsterdam-Noord, which was where the apartment was located. As our thrumming blue boat churned the coffee-colored water, I regarded the mysterious land for which we were bound with some trepidation. Behind us was Amsterdam Centraal, and beyond that the ring of canals, old buildings, museums, and coffee shops for which Amsterdam is famous. In front of us, on the other hand, was a forbidding landscape, sparsely developed save for a few forlorn-looking buildings. I had the eerie feeling we were en route to Amsterdam's Staten Island.

The most forlorn-looking building we were looking at, Dries explained, was the former headquarters of Shell, the oil company. Not too long ago, people in Amsterdam regarded Amsterdam-Noord with derision. Now, modern high-rise residential buildings were opening in Amsterdam-Noord, and creative companies like MTV (if you consider MTV to be creative, which is debatable) were opening offices in the area. This gentrification theme was starting to sound really familiar: Amsterdam-Noord, Shoreditch in London, the Lagerhuset in Gothenburg, pretty much every place in Brooklyn . . . It seemed like in any place I went lately the pattern of "urban renewal" was the same. I wasn't sure if this meant that I was a completely typical post-gentrification urbanite, or that if you follow the bicycle you'll inevitably wind up someplace gentrified, or if every city in the world is being completely gentrified, or just some combination of the three.

In just a couple of minutes the ferry docked at Amsterdam-Noord, and the race to disembark began. I was immediately transported back to my BMX days as all the bicycles and scooters lined up at the gate of the ferry as if waiting for a heat to begin. As soon as the boat made contact with the dock and the gate went down they were off, dispersing into the mysterious lands beyond the ferry landing. Forced to walk with us, Dries led us along a paved path and through a construction site. The sky was gray, the wind was blustery, and the people on bicycles passed us as though we were standing still. It wasn't a long walk from the ferry landing to our building, but having a bicycle was clearly the difference between a five minute walk and a one minute ride. A visitor to New York or London could never touch a bike during his stay yet never feel that absence; here, the message was "You need to be on a bike!" I felt like the one kid at the pool party who's not wearing a bathing suit.

I needed a bike. Fast.

Finally, we arrived at our pleasingly modern high-rise, where, Dries installed us in our pleasingly modern apartment. He then departed, at which point we immediately set out to score some bikes.

I had a line on somebody who was going to provide us with a bakfiets (the fabled SUV of smugness) but the sad fact was I couldn't wait that long and we had errands to do. So we headed back to the ferry and went to a bike rental shop near the train station where, because we were Americans, they asked us if we needed bicycles with coaster brakes. This was not an unreasonable assumption on their part given the fact that Americans tend to view bicycles with the same mystification with which they view bidets, and I'm surprised they didn't also offer to install training wheels.

It wasn't too long before Sara and I were outfitted with matching step-through bikes, and we tested them out in front of the shop. Sara was quite comfortable on hers, though mine felt a bit too small, and the lack of reach to the handlebars coupled with the resultant twitchy handling made the act of steering it feel less like riding a bike and more like constantly hoisting a pair of pants. It also didn't help that Elliott was perched in a front-mounted child seat that appeared to date back to the oil crisis. (That's the 1970s oil crisis, not the one we're in now.)

Still, like a lot of American cyclists, I discovered cycling through recreation and thus I tend to be overly picky when it comes to equipment. This is probably one of our greatest handicaps as a cycling nation—the complete inability to simply jump on any bike and ride. Instead, having been reared in a country where cycling is primarily a recreational pursuit, the few of us who do actually ride can't so much as hop on a basic city bike without fussing over seat height and bar width and lamenting the lack of foot retention. It's like renting a beige Chevy econobox, criticizing the handling, and complaining about the lack of a five-point racing harness. Sure, the bike was not ideal, but it was also perfectly safe and completely rideable, and so I reminded myself to forget all my cycling preconditions and just ride.

It was the evening rush now, and Amsterdam's bicycle paths were teeming with commuters. I remember very clearly the first time I drove a car on the highway with my learner's permit. First there was the thrilling acceleration on the entrance ramp, and then that disconcerting merging sensation that always feels a bit like high-diving into a shallow pool no matter how many times you've checked behind you. Once I'd slotted into traffic, I was both excited and nervous, taking great pains to keep my speed steady, maintain the appropriate distance from the car in front of me, and not run afoul of any other drivers. Suddenly, I was part of this businesslike procession, and I felt acutely aware that I was really still just a child among grown-ups.

It was the same self-awareness I'd felt as a child in Penn Station, where I experienced for the first time what it was like to be among the throngs of purposeful commuters in their tan raincoats, my little legs rushing to keep up with their whooshing slacks and my hands ready to protect my eyes from those swinging pointy-cornered briefcases.

I'd nearly forgotten how novel that sensation of merging can be. Driving had become tedium, and the New York City transit system had ingested and passed me like an undigested corn kernel more times than I could possibly count. Now, however, as Sara and I merged onto the busy bicycle path by the Centraal Station, I experienced the thrill of the merge for the first time in years. People in business attire rode swiftly, purposefully, and closely. Just as I had learned on the Southern State Parkway all those years ago, I knew that to slow suddenly or to turn erratically would at best anger my fellow commuters or at worst cause an accident. I rode diligently and attentively—not only did I have my young son perched on my handlebars but I also had my national cycling pride riding on my shoulders, and there was no way I was going to Clark W. Griswold this situation by brake-checking a Dutchman, causing a pileup, and winding up beneath three metric tons of sensible commuter bikes.

You might think riding in Dutch rush hour is like riding in a paceline, but it's not. Sure, in a paceline the slightest misstep is liable to end in disaster. Also, in a paceline anything can happen. In a race I once watched someone roll over a stick, and his wheel sent it cartwheeling through the air like that bone in the opening scene from *2001: A Space Odyssey.* The stick then landed right in the spokes of a rider a few bikes ahead of me, launching him over the handlebars like he was Peter Dinklage sharing a seesaw with James Gandolfini.

But riding among the Amsterdamers wasn't like riding in a paceline. Despite the skill involved, a paceline is still recreation, and if unpredictable things happen, everybody is at least going in the same direction. Riders aren't constantly merging in and out of a race, and you're not dealing with other races that are headed in a different direction. Sure, riding in a paceline is certainly more *difficult*, and it's also much faster, but as far as random interactions among strangers engaged in the simple act of going one place to the other, this was perhaps the most physical and well-orchestrated bike ride of which I'd ever been a part.

Indeed, I'd been in Amsterdam for only a day, and already I'd had a revelation: despite being a seasoned cyclist by American standards, I'd never experienced an actual bicycle rush hour. I've raced bikes for years; I've ridden with professionals; I've worked as a bike messenger and commuted in one of the largest cities in the entire world; I even write about bikes for a *living*. Yet here I was amazed and even slightly intimidated by something to which a typical Dutch grandmother probably wouldn't give so much as a second thought.

We don't have a bicycle rush hour. Instead, we have, at most, bunches of five or ten bicycle commuters who wind up at the red light at the same time. Moreover, since our formative cycling years were stolen from us, most adults in America who have rediscovered cycling are still in the "Wheee! I'm on a bike!" phase. We race each other over bridges on the way to work. We crash into each other. We wear absurd getups, and our commuting wardrobes are strange hybrids of racewear and street clothes that make us look like regular people who shared a teleport machine with club racers and got our DNA all scrambled like in the Jeff Goldblum remake of *The Fly*.

Even Portland, which is America's most enlightened cycling city, doesn't really have a bicycle rush hour—not like this. Sure, there are lots of bike commuters and bike lanes there, but for all that cycling infrastructure it's still very much Cycling American-Style. Besides the amenities, the main difference between Portland bike commuting and bike commuting in other cities is that Portlanders think they're better at it. Portland is the only place I've ever ridden where I've been yelled at by a stranger on a bike for not using proper hand signals.

Anyway, Sara, Elliott, and I made it to the supermarket without incident, stocked up on provisions, and returned to our temporary home by means of the ferry. All in all, the journey went very smoothly, except for the fact that it turned out I bought buttermilk instead of regular milk because I couldn't understand the writing on the carton and I was too embarrassed to ask anybody what it said.

As I stepped back into the elevator and prepared to head out into the rain in order to return to the store and get the right kind of milk I was joined by our new neighbor, a woman who appeared to be somewhere in her fifties. She looked me up and down and then uttered something in Dutch, so I told her I didn't understand her.

"Oh, sorry, I said something nasty," she explained, pausing for effect. "About the weather," she added by way of clarification.

After exchanging pleasantries we parted ways on the ground floor, and as I unlocked my rental bike she flew by on her own bike, completely undaunted by the rain, which was coming down pretty hard at this point. "Ah, like a real Dutch!" she exclaimed, pointing to my bike, and I was heartened by her approbation. I also realized that this was something else I'd almost never seen in all my years of city cycling—a woman in ordinary clothes simply riding off into the rain. Besides bike theft and motor vehicle traffic, inclement weather is perhaps the most oft-cited reason Americans give for not commuting by bike.

Apparently, it's not much of a reason.

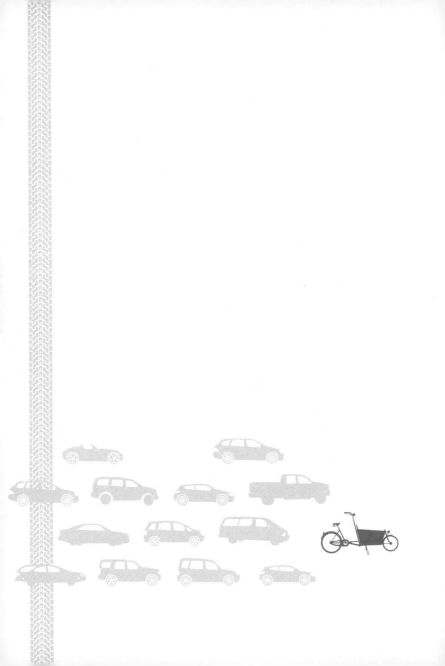

Chapter 9:

ALL ABOARD THE
FLOTILLA OF
SMUGNESS

A bakfiets is a cargo or freight bike, and with its large frontal trough for carrying sundries such as groceries and small humans it looks a bit like a rideable wheelbarrow.

Bakfiets and other variations on the cargo bike are common in places like Amsterdam and Copenhagen, but despite being a lifelong cyclist I wasn't really aware of them until a few years ago when they suddenly started popping up in the more smug neighborhoods of Brooklyn—you know, the ones lined with brownstones, organic grocers, and Subarus.

In New York City, cargo bikes are nothing new, and indeed Worksman Cycles in Queens has been supplying businesses with heavy-duty delivery bikes for over a hundred years. However, private use of these bicycles is a new phenomenon; as bicycle infrastructure began to expand and these smug neighborhoods inexplicably went from being wealthy to being extremely wealthy despite the fact that the economy was melting down like cheese in a fondue pot, I began to see people "portaging" children in imported bakfiets. Sure enough it wasn't long before papers like the *New York Times* were reporting on the phenomenon and publishing photo essays of fashionably dressed riders schlepping their towheaded offspring to private school.

"What new smuggery is this?" I asked myself disgustedly. "How do you even have one of these in the city unless you're loaded?" Indeed, who but the very wealthiest people could have not only the money for one of these behemoths but also the space necessary to store it? New York City is simply not a place you can park any sort of bicycle outdoors for any length of time, because if it doesn't get stolen it's almost certainly going to be removed by an irate building superintendent or simply smashed to bits by an inept parallel parker. And clearly leaving something like a bakfiets would invite a whole other level of mistreatment. For example, I used to own a motorcycle, and people used it as a public bench—I always used to return to it and find half-consumed meals and beverages on the seat. Surely the frontal tub of a bakfiets would provide a lovely spot for a nap, or even a perfect vessel to fill with water and bathe a dog.

Clearly, then, if these bakfiets had not been taken over by homeless people or itinerant dog groomers that meant their owners had room to store them inside, which meant they were rich, which in turn meant that I was jealous of them, and which ultimately manifested itself in my finding both them and their bakfietses incredibly annoying. Here, I told myself, were people with the luxury to make a conspicuous statement about environmentalism and sustainability with the latest smug Dutch status symbol, and who could afford to leave the Volvo at home while they shopped for organic groceries and posed for *New York Times* pictorials.

At the same time, in addition to resenting New York City's bakfiets riders for mostly superficial and judgmental reasons, I also resented the fact that New York City made it so difficult to have a cargo bike. Why should having such a practical means of conveyance be the exclusive domain of the landed gentry? My own cargo bike, the Big Dummy, was one of the great cycling revelations of my adult life, yet I was barely able to keep it—I just manage to fit it in a secret outdoor parking location next to my apartment building. This is just a longtail cargo bike, which is basically a mountain bike with a longer wheelbase. You could probably fit a Big Dummy *in* a bakfiets. Since I couldn't store it in my apartment, it was just dumb luck that I was able to store it safely outside. However, had I elected to purchase a giant SUV I'd have had little trouble parking it, since there's free on-street parking all over New York City. Really, it just didn't seem fair.

But I wasn't in Brooklyn anymore. I was in Holland. And like a college student visiting Amsterdam can't wait to hit the "coffee shops," I was itching to get my posterior on a bakfiets.

As it happens, some months prior I had made the acquaintance of a man named Henry Cutler. Originally from New York, Henry had moved to Amsterdam with his family and opened a bike shop called WorkCycles, and when I told him we would be in Amsterdam he was kind enough to offer to furnish us with bikes. It had been intermittently rainy and persistently gray ever since we arrived in Amsterdam, but WorkCycles—located in the Jordaan district—was the sort of place that made you feel as though you were someplace sunny. Between the exposed brick and the chalkboard "menu" it also made you feel as though you should be ordering brunch.

Most notably, though, there was also not a single racing bike or a stitch of Lycra in the place, nor were there any windbreaker-and-helmet-clad customers trying on sunglasses that they would later order on the Internet. There were just bakfiets the size of canoes, racks, capacious saddle bags, and sturdy city bikes that looked like they could survive a month at the bottom of an Amsterdam canal and emerge unscathed. Between the decor and the elegantly practical bicycles and accessories, this was the sort of shop that would make the bike activists of Brooklyn and Portland wet themselves and then collapse sobbing into their organic vegan couscous.

I too was impressed, and I was almost intimidated when Henry wheeled out the green and orange bakfiets I was going to be riding. Sure, I'd ridden in two Singlespeed World Championships and delivered modeling portfolios in hailstorms as a New York City bicycle messenger, but shoving off into the bike lanes of Amsterdam in a rolling log flue promised to be a completely new cycling experience. He showed me the operation of the center-stand (held in the "up" position by magnets underneath the plywood cargo box), explained the locking procedure (chain through the frame, then secure the rear wheel lock), and tutored me in the installation and removal of the clear weatherproof canopy. (Despite his instructions, the first time I did it one of the little retaining rods popped out and thwacked me pretty painfully in the nuts.) He also warned me that the bike would turn a bit more slowly than an ordinary bike, something I already expected from the geometry and truly "epic" wheelbase. The thing was big. Straddling the bicycle, I was still in Henry's shop in the Jordaan, but the front wheel seemed to be somewhere in Belgium.

In addition to the bakfiets, he also set Sara up with a purple and pink city bike quite a bit more attractive and nimble than the ones we had rented. Then, we sat Elliott on a bench in the bakfiets, strapping him into his little safety harness and closing the canopy. Finally, once we were all situated, we set out with Henry on his own bakfiets. He had his daughter (a few months younger than Elliott) in tow and we were accompanying them to pick up his young son (a couple of years older than Elliott) from school so we could get the full familial Dutch cycling experience.

The first thing I noticed about the bakfiets was that it did indeed turn slowly—very slowly. In fact, it didn't turn so much as it tilted vertically on its axis, and if you wanted to initiate a directional change you had to think about it beforehand and swing out wide before diving into a turn; otherwise you were just going to tilt over like a beached rowboat. In mountain biking, the idea is not to "dab" (put your foot down) when negotiating technical sections of trail, and I'm sorry to report that on the bakfiets I was dabbing constantly. Once again, Amsterdam was reducing me to a total "noob." Of course, when you're riding off-road it's always a good idea to watch a better rider and follow his or her lines through the terrain, and so I did my best to follow and copy Henry, who handled his bakfiets so adeptly that he seemed to be able to hop it up curbs.

It wasn't long before I found myself getting used to the bakfiets, though, which is when I started noticing other stuff, like the fact that no drivers were beeping at me. Here I was piloting a bike the size of a Toyota Yaris, yet amazingly I didn't seem to be getting in anybody's way. More amazingly, nobody was asking me to account for myself (like that woman had on Vanderbilt Avenue back in Brooklyn), nor were pedestrians even remotely curious about or looking askance at the large human-powered contraption I was riding. Sure, I'd only ridden a few blocks, but by this point in New York City at least three people would have spat at me, and I'd also have been stopped by a *New York Times* photographer on yet another formulaic lifestyle piece about the gentrification of Brooklyn.

This is around when I started feeling legitimately amazed, which is where you found me at the very beginning of this book.

But while the cycling was idyllic, the weather was not. In fact, by this time it was raining rather heavily, which meant that I was soaking wet, and Sara was soaking wet. Elliott, however, was as dry as an English one-liner beneath the canopy of the bakfiets, muttering to himself happily just as he always did at home on the Big Dummy. As for Sara and me, we didn't really mind being wet, since being showered with water is vastly preferable to being showered with insults. Plus, it rains fairly often in New York too, which means you're often showered with both rain *and* insults. If anything, in New York, the worse the weather the less tolerant of cyclists the drivers are. It's like they don't think you should be out there in the rain or snow, and so they feel inclined to drive the lesson home by punishing you further.

After picking up Henry's son from school we all rode through a park and to a café, where we had one of those typical kiddie lunches that involve lots of goal-tending. Kiddie lunches have their own rhythm, and once you surrender to it, it's almost soothing—bend down to pick up the dropped spoon, sit up just in time to save your drink from being spilled, bend back down to pick up the fork, then back up to stop the kid from setting fire to the menu with the candle on the table, and so forth. Like anything repetitive, it's potentially transcendent, sort of like kneeling and standing in church, or davening in front of the Wailing Wall in Jerusalem. Also, one thing I'll say for America is that most dining establishments are rather tolerant of these sorts of scenarios, for while we may not indulge cyclists, indulging our children is a national pastime. I was relieved to find that the Dutch were tolerant of this too—at least the Dutch people who ran this particular establishment were. In London when we walked into a restaurant with a kid the staff generally looked at us like we were carrying roadkill and seated us accordingly.

By the way, in case you haven't been counting, our party consisted of three adults and three human children, not to mention bags and schoolbooks and diaper bags and other sundries. That's easily a minivan full of stuff, and we were able to transport ourselves around Amsterdam comfortably and swiftly on a grand total of three (3) bicycles. Sure, two of those bicycles were pretty large, but certainly not so large that it was difficult or obtrusive to park them on the sidewalk while we had lunch.

So our first afternoon of full-on familial cycling was extremely pleasant, and indeed it might even have rated as blissful had it not been for the rain. (It's hard to feel blissful when you're wearing damp pants.)

Still, as lovely as all of this was, I was also beginning to sense that something in Amsterdam was ever so slightly amiss. At first I hardly noticed it, in the same way you hardly notice that faint mildew smell in your new house because you're so taken with it, or how you gloss right over the fact that your new boyfriend or girlfriend says "supposably" instead of "supposedly" because you're just so smitten. However, once the initial infatuation wears off, these sorts of things come into sharp relief, and it isn't long before these hairline cracks grow into the giant fracture that causes the entire love affair to fail.

In this case, the mildew smell in Amsterdam was the motor scooters. (There's also an actual mildew smell, but it comes from the canals.) Imagine yourself riding along an Amsterdam bike path—swiftly, quietly, efficiently. Then imagine the weedwhacking sound of a two-stroke motor behind you, and then someone dressed kind of like Ali G zooming into your peripheral vision astride a motorized scooter. Then, imagine this person darting in front of you and filling your nostrils with his oily exhaust and his pheromone-infused body spray. It's a gross intrusion, like finding a hair in your wine or hearing Auto-Tune at the opera.

At first, it didn't really bother me, because in New York I'm often tailgated and then cut off in the bike lane by similarly unctuous characters, only they're in three-ton Escalades instead of on 250-pound scooters. Really, the size difference was almost laughable, and it's like fleeing a pack of stampeding elephants for years only to be attacked by a swarm of gnats—it's such a relief you almost welcome them.

However, while an elephant can crush you in a single step, gnats will slowly drive you mad with their constant nibbling, and in certain ways that's almost worse. As scooters kept zipping by me in the bike lane I could certainly see how, over time, they could transform me from a blissed-out bike lane denizen to an irascible, snarling lunatic. (Or, more accurately, *back* into an irascible, snarling lunatic, since that's pretty much my default mode.) Mainly though, I wondered *why* anybody would want to ride a scooter in the bike lane, when an engine of only 50cc can be sufficient to reach highway speeds, and they could just ride along with the cars.

Well, as we enjoyed our lunch Henry explained it all to me,

though I'll quote from his blog, bakfiets-en-meer.nl, rather than attempt to recount our dialogue:

Dutch "fietspaden" (bike paths and lanes) are not exclusively for the use of bicyclists. Also allowed are vehicles legally classified as "snorfietsen" (in principle slow, motor-assisted bicycles limited to 25 km/hr), as well as several types of small vehicles for disabled and elderly people. At least that was the original intention when the laws were created. It seems that nobody could imagine that anybody but an old lady would want to ride a moped without a helmet and be able to ride and park it anywhere.

Recently this loophole in the law has been exploited, primarily by the scooter manufacturers who make supposed reduced speed models that are registered as "snorfietsen" and may be ridden without helmets on the bike paths. They're called "snorscooters." Unlike the snorfietsen the laws are based on these are much bigger and have no (even vestigial) pedals. In fact, aside from a little, blue registration plate they're indistinguishable from the normal, fast scooters that are driven on the roads. Once in the hands of their new (mostly young) owner the speed limiter is quickly removed and the motor often hot-rodded to increase the maximum speed to several times the legal limit. The police, apparently preoccupied with evicting squatters and harassing various ethnic groups, don't enforce either the speed limits on the bike paths or the specifications of scooters. As a result snorscooters have exploded in popularity and generic, franchise-looking scooter stores are popping up throughout the city.

In learning all of this, two things struck me:

1) "Fietspaden," "snorfietsen," and "snorscooters" would all be perfect characters for my Dr. Seussian bike-themed children's book;

and

2) There's something about things with wheels that turns people into assholes.

Actually, as far as point number two goes, that's oversimplifying it a bit. The truth is that we're all inherently assholes, but the wheels just make it more pronounced. Really, wheels do the same thing for our inner asshole that alcoholic beverages do—they coax it out and imbue it with false confidence. In a lifetime of traveling on wheels I've experienced this phenomenon day after day, though it was only after having a son and spending lots of time in playgrounds that I noticed it's something innate that's programmed into our DNA. Just add a tricycle or a scooter or one of those rideable plastic cars into the mix and even the most fun-loving group of kids will turn on each other like little gamecocks. First, they fight for control of the vehicle, and then once someone wins and gets on it he tears around the playground baiting and taunting anybody who's foolish enough to come near him.

This behavior continues into adulthood, only the vehicles now have motors, so instead of just being like booze they're actually like booze mixed with some other pharmaceutical. Therefore the asshole effect is synergistic. In any case, I can only assume this is the science behind a physically able person riding a hopped-up scooter in a bicycle lane.

Once we'd finished lunch, we returned to our respective bakfietsen and made our way back to our respective homes, and every so often we'd see other parents on various two- or three-wheeled child-portaging contrivances making their school pickups. It was simply No Big Thing, and it was a relief from the block-long lines of double-parked cars and SUVs you'll find outside of a Brooklyn school. Of course, we drive our kids to school like this because we think it's safe, but as a result American streets are the transportation equivalent of Mutually Assured Destruction—the thinking is that if we're all getting around in vehicles large enough to crush a suburban ranch home, then we will attain Nash equilibrium and be forced to act in the interest of the group.

That evening, after putting Elliott to bed, Sara and I settled down to watch some TV. As we flipped through the channels, we realized everything was in Dutch, and as amusing as it is to watch people with heavily-gelled hair introduce incredibly cheesy music videos in a language you can't understand, eventually we pined for entertainment in our native tongue. So we rummaged around the apartment owner's DVD collection, in which we finally found something in English—a documentary called *What the Bleep Do We Know*.

According to Wikipedia, *What the Bleep Do We Know* is "a 2004 film that combines documentary-style interviews, computer-animated graphics, and a narrative that describes the spiritual connection between quantum physics and consciousness." It's a very strange movie, and it has the sort of stilted, low-budget production that makes it seem like a porno film—or, worse, something that was made for Canadian television. During the movie, the actress Marlee Matlin walks around Portland (yes, the city in America that loves bikes), and strange stuff keeps happening to her—not the usual strange stuff that happens to you in Portland, like bicycle soup vendors offering you bowls of chowder, but trippy quantum physics stuff, like some creepy smiling kid who keeps disappearing and reappearing on a basketball court as Marlee Matlin regards him with considerable nonplussitude.

Anyway, ultimately the theme of the movie is that we create our own reality, and to underscore this point the film talks about how when Columbus's ships first appeared on the horizon in the New World, the Indians didn't see them. This wasn't because the ships were stealthy, but rather because these giant boats were so far beyond anything the Indians had ever experienced that they simply couldn't mentally process them and thus literally couldn't see them. Instead, presumably they simply went about their business until the ships landed, the conquistadors deboated, and the locals could no longer ignore the smallpox and the blunderbusses in their faces.

I'm pretty sure I don't believe the thing about the Indians not seeing the ships. In fact, I'd be willing to bet they not only saw the ships but also asked many, many questions about them, such as "What the fuck are those things?" "Where the fuck did they come from?" and "How the fuck do we get them out of here?"

However, at the same time I got their point, and we do indeed create our own reality. Moreover, we often ignore awful truths because they're simply too ghastly to contemplate. In fact, as I watched Marlee Matlin ramble around Portland and encounter increasingly vexing situations, I realized that this explained a great deal about life in America. As I grew older and started cycling less for personal recreation and more for practical transportation and family fun, I became increasingly amazed at our unwillingness to acknowledge the motor vehicle-induced carnage on the streets. Why were my neighbors in Brooklyn suing the city to remove a new bike lane when hundreds of people a year were being flattened by drivers with impunity? Why is the delivery cyclist considered a menace when the driver who kills somebody merely "had an accident?" Why do we accept driving as a safe mode of transportation when the truth is it's pretty much the most dangerous way to get around?

It's because we're like those Indians, only our ships on the horizon are giant SUVs.

And not only are we blind to the destruction wrought by cars, but we've in turn become blind to pedestrians and cyclists. The most oft-cited reason drivers give for hitting cyclists is "I didn't see him." This should be an admission of guilt, since if you don't see something then you're not doing your job as a driver, but in practice in America it's actually an acceptable excuse. Cyclists are indeed invisible here—we're like Schrodinger's cat, a rolling paradox, and we only flicker into existence when an SUV finally makes contact with us.

I know I was blind to the destruction wrought by cars for most of my life, but now that I'm aware of it it's impossible to ignore. Every year the streets seem more grotesque to me, like in the movie *They Live* when "Rowdy" Roddy Piper puts on those glasses and can suddenly see the aliens and their propaganda. Everywhere I see drivers on cell phones, nudging their way into intersections, the grills of their Escalades towering over the heads of pedestrians. And for the most part, we just accept this as The Way It Is. To point out the absurd imbalance and the resulting death toll borders on heresy. We're oddly comfortable with the idea that the small living things should yield to the giant debt machines on wheels, just as we used to be with the idea that the sun revolves around the Earth. And anybody who doesn't drive a car will find himself or herself excommunicated from the transportation infrastructure.

The Dutch, however, seem to have seen the ships coming, and they managed to fight them off—or at least to keep them under control.

Certainly this was partially an accident of geography (the Netherlands is about the size of Maryland, and the terrain is as flat as a Midwestern accent), but clearly there's something else going on too, and it's tempting to call it "humanity."

The Dutch always rode bikes, but in the post–World War II years of prosperity they became car-centric, just like us. Fewer people rode, more people drove, and unsurprisingly, more people died. But unlike us, the Dutch people didn't stand for it. Maybe they're just different from us, or maybe they'd been cycle-centric recently enough in their past that people remembered it was better, but for whatever reason the people demanded change, and they got it. Cycling went back up, driving went back down, and it's now so safe that if you wear a helmet on a bike they think there's something wrong with you.

In any case, I felt in Amsterdam like I used to when I was a child and we'd visit relatives in Florida in winter. Being able to go outside without first getting bundled up seemed impossibly novel, tremendously liberating, and almost otherworldly. But as great as it was to swim in December, riding a bike without feeling like a cockroach at a dinner party felt even better. For a New Yorker, it was somewhere between eating a California burrito and walking on a planet with a slightly weaker gravitational field.

"Why can't we have this at home?" I found myself wondering, just as I usually did in California while burying my face in a burrito the size of a baby's head. "It's just so simple!"

But while a burrito is pretty simple, I suppose happy cycling is not. One is mostly just a question of ingredients, while the other is apparently a matter of physics, and right now cycling in America is in a state of quantum entanglement.

Chapter 10:

SMUGNESS INTERRUPTUS

Sara, Elliott, and I were adjusting quite nicely to life in Amsterdam. Jet lag was a distant memory. Our Amsterdam-Noord apartment was comfortable and spacious, and hopping onto our bikes and taking the ferry into Amsterdam proper was becoming a matter of routine. Most importantly, life without vehicular oppression was agreeing with us. Our teeth were whiter, my bald spot had disappeared, and each of us had grown about four inches taller.

Well, that last sentence isn't true, but we were feeling pretty good.

Unfortunately, just as we were beginning to find our groove, I had to go back to London—alone. I had told my British publisher that I was going to be in the area (naïvely before leaving New York I had considered Amsterdam to be "in the area," as though going back and forth between the two was like commuting from Brooklyn to Manhattan), and so they went ahead and booked me as a guest on a BBC radio show called *Loose Ends*. Apparently, I was going to be on with actor John Hurt and lyricist Sir Tim Rice, as well as some other people who were considerably more accomplished than me. I was surprised to be in such distinguished company, especially since I'm used to being the guy who's interviewed on the local NPR affiliate for four minutes and fields questions from callers like "What's the deal with those recumbent bicycles?" I was honored to be invited, but I also suspected the show would be like a bottle of blended whiskey—full of aged ingredients and ultimately sleep-inducing.

Ideally, I would have liked to have taken a train all the way from Amsterdam to London in order to get what I imagined would be the "full Euro experience." However, that seemed like it would have taken too much time, so I flew instead, but when you factor in security and delays it probably took just as much time as the train. Plus, I forfeited the glamour of international rail travel, and had to settle for the woman sitting across from me on the train to Schiphol airport who had a giant cold sore on her lip, wore a pair of thigh-high leather boots, and spoke sensually on her cell phone in a language I could not readily identify. I imagined that she worked in the Amsterdam red-light district but was on her way back to the former Eastern Bloc country that was her home, where she would use her earnings to purchase a giant house, eight flat-screen TVs, and a Mercedes. No doubt the reality was far more prosaic.

While I was not relishing a trip across the North Sea that would separate me from my family during our blissful period of Total Smugness Immersion, I was looking forward to the opportunity to finally try the London bike-share system (or, more accurately, the

"Barclays Cycle Hire scheme"), and it says a lot about me that riding the so-called "Boris bikes" (named after their champion, London mayor Boris Johnson) was my idea of "cutting loose" on a solo London adventure. So after taking a train and a plane and another train I finally arrived exhausted at Victoria Station, and I stumbled outside in search of a bike like a drunk looking for a urinal.

My plan was to hire a bike and ride it to my hotel in Bloomsbury, only I had no idea where to find a bike-share kiosk, nor did I have any idea how to get to Bloomsbury. Fortunately, it turns out that all you have to do to find a bike-share kiosk is just pick a direction and walk, since the things are pretty much everywhere (at least in the more central parts of London). Getting to Bloomsbury was going to be a bit harder, though, since I had no knowledge of London, and looking at a street map of the city is like contemplating a bowl of spaghetti.

Plus, I didn't even have a map. I'd been carrying around an "A to Z" guide with me in my back pocket, but it seemed to have fallen out somewhere between Centraal and Victoria stations.

But first things first—it was time to rent a bike. I'd secretly been dreading this because I have a deep-seated fear of automated ticketing machines that is second only to my fear of revolving doors, and I feel the same pressure when I stand in front of an airport boarding pass dispenser or train station ticketing machine that I do when people ask me for directions. The source of my dread is that everything's a yes or no question with a machine, and I prefer the subtle nuances and give-and-take of human interaction. (At least when it comes to ticketing; otherwise I prefer to be left alone.) Buying from a machine is like taking a multiple-choice test on Scantron, which was probably my least favorite thing about school after gym class. I happen to be one of those people who can read too deeply into almost anything, and so I have a very hard time with straightforward questions. "What do you mean by 'Are you checking any bags?'" I ask myself as I contemplate the screen, and before I know it people are yelling at me and the machine has eaten my credit card.

Fortunately, the bike share kiosk was very straightforward as these things go, apart from the twenty-something pages of "terms and conditions" that I declined to read and that almost certainly prevented anybody from suing Barclays should I plummet into the Thames or wind up underneath a double-decker bus. I swiped my card, the kiosk spat out a receipt with a number on it, I punched that number into the wheel lock, and then I pulled the bike out, at which point I was free to get as lost or dead as I wanted.

If my first rental bike in Amsterdam had been somewhat less than ideal from a bike snob perspective, the Boris bike had the aesthetics of a handicapped toilet. Nevertheless, there was something exhilarating about its utilitarian ugliness, and my utter lack of responsibility for the care of the machine. (Apart from my responsibility to return it to a bike-share kiosk on time, since if I didn't Barclays would charge me something like a billion dollars.) Finally, the bicycle had been transformed into something totally practical and completely devoid of charm, like an umbrella or a shopping cart, and had been so divorced from materialization, fetishization, and customization that it didn't even have an owner. You could now be a bike commuter in London without even owning a bicycle, and that was a beautiful thing. Adjusting the saddle height, I threw a leg over the Boris bike and set off in the general direction in which I guessed Bloomsbury lay.

In addition to looking like a handicapped toilet the Boris bike handled like one too, but it moved and it stopped and was otherwise perfectly serviceable. Without my street map I was forced to use my phone's GPS, though since I didn't want to incur costly overseas data charges, I didn't leave it on and instead rode until I got lost again, at which point I'd allow myself a brief glimpse of the phone just to get back on track. It was a pretty stupid way of getting around—like only opening your eyes every ten minutes for five seconds at a time—but I did eventually wind up where I needed to be.

This was also my first time actually riding a bicycle in London, and apart from not knowing where I was going it felt oddly comfortable in that it was very much like riding a bicycle in New York City. Lots of car traffic, lots of pedestrians, the odd fellow cyclist on a fixed-gear, in road kit, or in Day-Glo safety attire . . . Really, the main difference between riding in London and riding in New York seemed to be one of intensity, with London a bit shy of New York in that department. Even today, riding a bike in New York is still a lot like what I remember a 1980s hardcore show to be—deafening volume, barely-controlled chaos, and no shortage of bodily contact. Riding a bike in London was like going to the same show while wearing earplugs and some light padding. The taxi drivers in particular seemed more genteel in their driving style, and there was a distinct lack of giant SUVs playing window-rattling music and driven by people with breadloaf-sized rolls of neck fat who made no secret of their desire to kill you. I'm sure there's a London-area equivalent of this driver, but I was fortunate enough not to encounter him.

One other key difference between New York and London was in the cycling infrastructure itself. Like New Yorkers, Londoners have also been clamoring for bike infrastructure for quite some time. However, besides the whole bike-share thing, they've gotten a whole lot less than we have. The bike lanes in London are a lot like that naked Indian in Oliver Stone's *The Doors* in that they'd suddenly materialize, I'd try to follow them, and then they'd disappear as quickly as they appeared. In fact, in lieu of bike lanes, London has a lane of traffic that is dedicated to buses, taxis, and bicycles. This seems counterintuitive in that in New York the buses and taxis are the last vehicles you'd want to share a lane with, but it didn't work as badly as I thought it would—apart from having to suck down bus exhaust.

Ultimately, I suspected that the real difference between New York and London is that in London you don't have to dig nearly as deep to find the beating heart of courtesy, and this was embodied by the zebra crossings. I'd watch with amazement as vehicles of all kinds would come to a halt for pedestrians in zebra crossings, even in the throes of rush hour, and it was an indication to me that London still has not completely surrendered the notion that an unprotected and self-propelled human should take priority. I couldn't imagine such a thing in New York, where the de facto expectation is that traffic has the right of way and people in the street are expected to scurry for cover like squirrels.

Early the next morning, a minivan with my name in the window picked me up at my hotel and drove me the roughly seventy-five yards to the BBC. On the way I noticed that the bike-share kiosk at which I had docked my bike the night before was completely empty, and I can only assume the reason for this was that all the people who had crowded the pubs the night before had used them to get home. Upon arriving at the BBC I noticed a group of people standing around holding little booklets, which seemed surprising to me given how early it was. I assumed they must be part of a tour group, but Gideon Coe, the cohost of *Loose Ends* who interviewed me, later explained to me that they were probably autograph-seekers waiting for John Hurt. The idea of a bunch of middle-aged people standing around in the early morning waiting for John Hurt's autograph seemed impossibly earnest to me, and as accomplished an actor as he is, I'd imagine the most he'd get in New York would be the occasional comment from a passerby. "Hey, aren't you the guy from *Captain Correlli's Mandolin*?" Then again, I was oddly tempted to get his autograph myself, since he's been in no fewer than two Mel Brooks movies, which is about as great an achievement as it's possible for me to imagine.

In any case, as I sat in the studio and we all went through our respective spiels, I contemplated just how strange it was that I was on the radio with a famous actor and a famous lyricist for the simple reason that I write about riding bikes. It felt especially odd considering I had just come from Amsterdam, where the act of cycling was so completely *ordinary*. They might as well have been interviewing me about using the bathroom. Don't get me wrong, I was relishing the experience, but that didn't make it any less odd. As the show's other cohost, Clive Anderson, bantered with Sir Tim Rice about his work on *The Lion King* or something, I started experiencing something of a miniature crisis. Here I had concocted an entire persona and indeed something one might charitably call a "career" out of the boneheadedly simple act of cycling—something about as remarkable in Amsterdam as fetching the mail. John Hurt had played the Elephant Man; Tim Rice wrote *Jesus Christ Superstar*; the other guest whose name I don't remember was a chef and could cook the shit out of some food. Meanwhile, I had a blog about why riding a bike in New York sucks. Most distressingly, if my greatest cycling dream—the complete normalization and mainstreamification of cycling—were to come true, I'd probably be out of a job. Really, my entire schtick depended on the marginalization of cycling. What kind of a hypocrite was I?

After the show, the guests and show staff adjourned to a nearby pub, where we all enjoyed noontime beers and conversation beneath a photograph of Ned Sherrin. As I chatted with Gideon, and the guy from *1984* held court in his tweed blazer at the other end of the table, I realized I was as close as I'd ever been to my childhood fantasy of what England must be like: woody bars, intelligent conversation, wry humor, tweed . . . It was very satisfying. Then, after a while, everybody dispersed, and I set off into the sunny early afternoon with time to spare before my flight, reveling in the tidy townhouses and boutique retail and dining establishments. I wandered in this state of bliss until I came across a bike-share kiosk, at which point I grabbed a bike and rode until I could no longer ignore my powerful need to urinate. Then I docked it, darted into a café, darted back out, and undocked another one. The whole pluck-a-bike-from-the-trees nature of the bike-share program was really starting to win me over. Even one of the people from the BBC said he commuted by bike every single day exclusively by bike-share. In fact, he didn't even own a bike. Fixed-gear riders may talk about "Zen," but I can't think of anything more Zen than being a cyclist who doesn't own a bike—even if that bike has a bank's name plastered all over it.

Eventually, I found my way to Victoria station, and after doing the whole train-plane-train thing again for the second time in twenty-four hours I was finally back "home" in Amsterdam. It did feel like home, too, and as glamorous as London had been with its aging celebrities and its complimentary BBC preshow sandwiches and, its handicapped toilets on wheels, it was comforting to be back in this wetter, smaller, frumpier, and more intimate city. It was like easing into a pair of sweatpants. As my train pulled into Centraal Station, I reveled in the now-familiar sights through the rain-splattered window—the acres of bikes, the crooked buildings, the dirty canals—and I watched nervously as bolts of lightning struck somewhere in the vicinity of "our" apartment. It was Saturday night, and so I had to make my way through throngs of wet, drunken revelers in order to get to the ferry, which despite the tempest was punctual as usual and deposited me on the other side without incident.

I was beginning to see how London and Amsterdam had given birth to New York. Like London, New York is a cultural and financial capital, yet like Amsterdam it has a certain informality and unshaven lack of pretense. While the pace of London is immediately familiar to a New Yorker, the city doesn't evoke Greenwich Village or certain parts of Brooklyn in the way that Amsterdam does. If I had to choose between living with one parent or the other, I wondered which one I'd choose. It was a tough question, but neither was a bad proposition.

Chapter 11:

SWEPT AWAY

Sometime during our stay in Amsterdam, Sara, Elliott, and I took a little road trip with Henry and his kids. Arriving at his house in the Jordaan, we loaded up the bakfietses with children and provisions and headed off for a ride along the Amstel River.

Thanks to the growing bicycle infrastructure in New York, you can sort of feel comfortable on a bike in some parts of the city, and thanks to the lighter traffic and slower pace, you can sort of feel comfortable on a bike outside of the city. However, in between—in the urban-to-suburban transitional zone, where I grew up—it's pretty much a cycling nightmare. Unless you know the secret wormholes, you'll find that riding a bicycle from the city to what passes for the "country" is like punching your way out of a wet cardboard box inside of another wet cardboard box inside of yet another wet cardboard box inside of a piñata. This is because the outlying areas of New York City have all the crowding of the more cosmopolitan parts of the city with none of the walkability. These are America's first suburbs, and they've hardened into something like the brown crust around the edges of an egg when you've fried it too long. On top of that you've got Robert Moses's network of parkways and expressways that spit cars from their exit ramps onto the streets like a pan spits hot oil. (As you might have guessed by now, I'm pretty bad at cooking eggs.) Escape on a bike is only possible in those areas that are sheltered by accidents of geography, or were spared because Robert Moses's vision was never fully realized.

Leaving Amsterdam by bike was, unsurprisingly, a completely painless proposition, and breaking free of the city's ring of canals was effortless. The roads weren't barriers to bicycle travel like the roads I'm used to are; instead, they were more like gentle waves helping us out to sea. Sure, Amsterdam is not even remotely as big as New York, but it's still a pretty big town with something like a million people in it. Just try getting out of almost any American city big enough to have an airport or a sports team and sooner or later you're bound to wind up at an expressway wondering how to get past the damn thing. The only remotely New York–like part of our ride was when we passed through the Philips Electronics office park, and only in that it seemed like the sort of complex you might find in Garden City, Long Island. Otherwise, the city simply gave way to rustic houses and windmills and crew teams rowing along the Amstel until we found ourselves in a little riverside town where we had lunch.

Along the way we saw plenty of recreational cyclists on road bikes, though almost none were riding the stratospherically expensive bikes you usually see in America. In years of traveling New

York City's heavily-trafficked "roadie corridor" over the George Washington Bridge and up to Nyack, I've seen stunning displays of velocipedal opulence that make the spot where I keep my wallet ache. Carbon wheelsets costing thousands of dollars inserted into pro replica frames, their quick-release skewers jarringly askew; rotund triathletes in teardrop helmets hunched awkwardly over exotic aerobars, wobbling in the crosswind and pedaling with the choppy inefficiency of a malfunctioning eggbeater; middle-aged men with thousand-dollar wattage meters on their bikes and accompanied by a professional coach. Of all these extravagances, perhaps that last one is the most shocking to me. Despite the fact that people spend tens of thousands of dollars on their bicycles, you can at least rationalize it by pointing out that actually riding the thing is free. However, as coaching becomes more and more popular, amateur racers desperate to divest themselves of as much money as possible have finally figured out how to get charged for the simple act of riding by hiring coaches. If you're going to pay by the mile for your bike rides, you might as well just skip the coach and throw your bike in the trunk of a yellow cab.

Anyway, Henry explained to me that the overequipped middle-aged dilettante really doesn't exist in the Netherlands, since when it comes to supporting competitive riding the focus is on young and promising riders who actually have a chance at success. (It's quite the opposite in America, where teams consisting of thirty- and forty-something Category 3s and 4s expect equipment sponsorship and deep discounts at their local bike shop.) During my time in Amsterdam and especially on this particular ride I could certainly see the evidence that Henry was right. The typical older road cyclists wore pro team uniforms (a major fashion faux pas in the United States), rode modest bicycles with metal frames and metal wheels that had clearly been in service for a number of years, slipped effortlessly into echelons when the winds picked up (even among racers you'd be hard-pressed to find a rider in the United States who knows how to ride in an echelon), and spun their hairy calves in a velvety smooth manner that implied they could easily rip your legs off.

I suppose there's no need to go broke playing pro racer in a country where the bicycle is actually taken seriously and is a bold pattern in the national tapestry. Meanwhile, in America, a bicycle is generally seen as either a piece of exercise equipment or a mode of transport for people with an "alternative" sensibility, and so naturally our relationship with our bikes is a complicated one. We can be forgiven for overcompensating, or attempting to legitimize the enterprise by spending lots of money on it. ("Who are you beeping at? My bike cost more than your car!") Also, this behavior is not at all unique to cycling. There's just something in human nature that compels us to throw ourselves into our hobbies like rats into a bathtub full of chocolate sauce, and to spend all of our disposable income in the process.

I should add that this behavior extends to the hobby of travel, and I was certainly binging American-style. We'd only been overseas for about a week, but already I was renouncing my home country and "going native" (at least from a cycling perspective). I could feel myself becoming unbearably smug, and I knew that when I did finally return to New York I'd become one of those "In Amsterdam" types— you know, those annoying people who need to remind you how much better something is somewhere else. "You know, in Amsterdam people just ride in the rain without making a big deal about it." "You know, in Amsterdam people don't need fancy bikes." "You know, in Amsterdam every day is 'Bike to Work Day.'" And so forth.

Barf.

I especially realized this when we returned home from our road trip that evening, our bakfiets laden with groceries (we stopped at the market) and a sleeping Elliott. Really, the entire trip was exactly the opposite of Joseph Conrad's *Heart of Darkness*, and the adorable image of all the kids sharing Henry's bakfiets tub on the ride home was still fresh in my mind. Turning on my computer, I checked in on the latest American cycling news, and learned that a kerfuffle had erupted in Portland over the city's streetcar tracks. Apparently, cycling advocates were claiming that they made the streets too dangerous for cyclists. Some commenters even thought they should be removed. Apparently, the issue had come to a head when Fred Armisen, star of the show *Portlandia*, had stated that, were he to move to Portland, he would not become a bicycle commuter because he was afraid of riding over the streetcar tracks.

Day after day I'd been watching Amsterdamers of all ages and walks of life easily negotiate wet tram tracks on their bicycles while talking on cell phones, holding umbrellas over their heads, or carrying bags of groceries, and here was what is ostensibly America's most bike-savvy and velo-progressive city claiming that they were an insurmountable obstacle for cycling. At this point I wondered if there was any hope for American cycling, or if we'd just continue to constantly invent new prerequisites for using bicycles as transportation. Having outsourced most of our manufacturing, it seemed as though our chief national export was rapidly becoming the fabrication of elaborate, high-quality excuses:

—I'd ride, except it's too hot;

—I'd ride, except it's too cold;

—I'd ride, except my bike would get stolen;

—I'd ride, except I can't show up to work sweaty;

—I'd ride, except I'm scared of the tram tracks.

And so forth.

I mean, if even Portlanders couldn't deal with tram tracks, what hope did the rest of us have?

Nevertheless, my outrage was almost entirely born of my inflamed smugness, and clearly in my short time in Amsterdam I'd become delusional and insufferably self-righteous. Really, it makes sense that our cycling advocates are as outlandish as our recreational cyclists, and that they adopt causes and issues as exuberantly as roadies buy new components. Fred Armisen complains about the tram tracks and the advocates say, "Those! Let's get rid of those!" while the Cat 4 racer sees a new power meter and says, "That! I need that!"

Actually, the more I thought about it, the more I realized how similar Portland and Amsterdam actually are. They're both pretty flat, they're both pretty wet, and they've both got a sense of scruffy individuality. Also, they both love bikes, though Amsterdam's love is a more mature one while Portland's is still in the adolescent, hormonally charged, "public display of affection" phase. I wondered if maybe Amsterdam was a vision of what Portland will be like in a hundred years when it finally gets over itself.

I suppose only time will tell. Maybe by then people won't be afraid to ride on streetcar tracks anymore.

Our time in Amsterdam was drawing to a close, and we were going to miss the place.

While I was in London, Sara and Elliott had spent the day riding around with an American friend of Sara's who had relocated to Amsterdam-Noord, and in so doing she'd become familiar with the area. So, as sort of a farewell, we set off on a tour. Our somewhat desolate industrial area yielded to a suburban neighborhood which in turn gave way to winding streets lined with little houses that overlooked the water. In its quaint marshiness it reminded me of Bayswater.

As we continued on, bike paths ran through lush pastures grazed upon by sheep, and the sun and the wind gave the grass the vibrant, swirly effect you see in all those Van Gogh paintings. We were really only a few miles from the canal rings of Amsterdam, but our surroundings were surprisingly pastoral, and I couldn't help imagining ourselves living here.

But there was no way I could live here, for as I'd realized during that BBC radio show, what I did and who I was was simply not valid in Amsterdam. At best I'd be the Yakov Smirnoff of the Netherlands. ("In Netherlands, truck stop for bike. In America, truck stop *on* bike!") I also had to admit I liked that feeling you get in both New York and London, the thrill that comes with existing in a city that drives trends, commerce, popular culture, and finance—even if most of the time it's driving those things pretty heedlessly and winds up wrapping them around a tree.

Certainly Amsterdam had once been one of these cities, but in the last few hundred years it had come to its senses and settled down. It was now a great and beautiful city full of culture and history, and in which it was actually possible to travel by bicycle without feeling like you might be killed by one of your neighbors. It seemed a place that was very comfortable with its humanity, and it was this more than anything we'd miss. In Amsterdam we were outsiders in every way—we didn't speak the language, we didn't know our way around, and we really had no business being there other than simply wanting to be—and yet as a family that likes to travel by bicycle we could move about easily and comfortably, and in so doing we'd been able to do everything from run errands to explore the countryside in a way that, in a short amount of time, made us feel perfectly at home. Meanwhile, I'd lived in New York my entire life yet still felt like an outsider as soon as I got on a bike. Why? Because a good number of my neighbors objected to my two-wheeled presence, and saw me as an obstacle robbing them of a few more precious inches for their SUVs.

It was like our lives were a form of currency, and we were returning to a place where that currency had a far lower value. It was a depressing thought, and I'd like to think one day in America we can enjoy a more favorable exchange rate.

chapter 12:

WELCOME BACK

Sara has sort of a Dutch-style bicycle that she uses to get around Brooklyn. We usually leave it in our building's parking lot, but shortly after returning from Amsterdam she left it for one night chained to a signpost on the street in front of the neighbors' building. When she returned to it the next morning, the building's superintendent told her it was a good thing she showed up because he was about to cut it off.

We were home.

One of the most fascinating aspects of travel is the way your home feels when you come back to it. When I returned from India, where I visited New Delhi, I remember walking through midtown Manhattan during rush hour and thinking it felt as placid and orderly as a small village. It was a little different returning from London and

Amsterdam, and when I set out into the city for the first time since I returned, my reaction was basically this:

"God, people are such *assholes* here!"

Probably the saddest thing I've seen in a while was watching a driver intentionally peel out in a crosswalk near the school on my block; kids were still making their way to school, and the crossing guard was almost completely enveloped in putrid blue smoke.

Not only do we accept this kind of behavior and the deaths that come with it, but we then turn around and advocate for the prosecution of cyclists. In fact, one of the biggest anti-cycling pitches in New York City is that scofflaw cyclists are a threat to children. Before visiting Amsterdam I wondered why so many of my neighbors consider bicycles a menace to children when the fact is they only possess a tiny fraction of the sheer child-killing power of the automobile, which is the leading cause of child deaths in the city. Finally, though, I realized what it was:

We hate weak stuff.

Yes, there's one thing Americans despise more than anything else—including dead children—and that's weakness. Bicycles are weak, and cars are strong. Therefore, we can live with our children getting killed by strong stuff like cars and guns (which happens all the time), but the very thought of one dying because of some wimp on a bike (which happens basically never) is an affront to our sensibilities. It's perfectly fine to die in America, just as long as you do it like a man.

Nevertheless, I continued to ride with Elliott, and as it happens our return to New York more or less coincided with the start of the Occupy Wall Street protests.

When I was a teenager I was very political. Actually, that's not true—it was more that I liked bands that were political, and so I adopted protest as a sort of affectation. I even started a grassroots organization called UCAW, or "United Citizens Against War." Sure, the name wasn't exactly catchy (it sounded more like a sound a chicken might make), but it at least fulfilled the prerequisite of having an A in it that I could render as an anarchy sign.

As for which war UCAW was united against, it wasn't just one war but all wars, and I struck my first blow when I made a flyer. First, I drew a logo in the scratchy handwritten style popular with the peace punk bands I used to go see in the Lower East Side at the time. Then, I cut out some photos of war atrocities from *Time* magazine as sort of an homage to Dead Kennedys artist Winston Smith. After that I typed up some antiwar prose on my mom's typewriter, and then I finally scraped some loose change together and photocopied the whole mess at the public library. Sadly, I got bored after that, and so UCAW remained a short-lived organization of one, which is why war still exists today. I'm glad there was no Internet back then—partially because it taught me the value of working with my hands, but mostly because if there had been an Internet I might have posted my flyer on Facebook and it might still exist somewhere to humiliate me.

As the years went on my antiestablishment affectations began to fade, and I also grew increasingly skeptical of other antiestablishment people, mostly because I suspected they were probably about as clueless as I had been. Plus, I felt as though I was suitably detached from the "establishment" as it was, since I'd spent pretty much my entire adult life working for the sorts of small book-related businesses that tend not to do stuff like dump oil into the ocean or employ child labor. Basically, I felt that in living my life on my own terms I was holding true to my childhood ideals, and that anything more than that amounted to the equivalent of carving anarchy signs into my desk at school.

Nevertheless, my trip to Amsterdam had put me in a much more questioning frame of mind with regard to my home, and so I wasn't quite so dismissive of the whole Occupy Wall Street thing. Shortly after our return, Elliott and I rode to the Manhattan Bridge for one of our trainspotting sessions. (Watching subway trains roar over the Manhattan Bridge is an excellent form of free childhood entertainment, plus it's more edifying than going to Chuck E. Cheese.) As we watched the Q train rattle its way to Brooklyn, I looked across the river and thought, "Maybe we should head into Manhattan and see what's going on." So we joined the late afternoon traffic heading south down Broadway and went to Zuccotti Park.

The park was an odd mix of urgency and leisure, with some people exchanging signs and talking hurriedly as others reclined on dirty mattresses reading political books or eating Cheez-Its. Also, there were bikes—lots of bikes. Police and reporters stood on the periphery, and people who might be spectators or protestors or maybe a little bit of both wandered through the park. I was one of these wanderers, wheeling Elliott along on the Big Dummy and experiencing a wave of mixed feelings. On one hand, the klatches of people dressed like sixties revolutionaries or clutching folk instruments seemed kind of silly, but on the other hand here was an entire park full of people who had come together through the potent combination of profound dissatisfaction and the Internet. Most importantly, they were saying something that needed to be said—even if many of them went shirtless as they said it, or had trouble expressing it without bongo drum accompaniment.

When I was barely old enough to walk, my mother took me to an anti-nukes rally. I had no idea what nukes were, except that they were apparently something very bad, and only walking slowly with signs could stop them. I remember almost nothing of the protest apart from feeling lost in a denim-barked forest of legs, but that cloying sensation of being in a huge, chanting crowd stayed with me. That may be why I was never compelled to repeat it (nor was my mother; I'm pretty sure that remains her only protest), but it's a memory I'm glad to have. So as Elliott and I picked our way through the Occupy protesters in their various states of undress, I wondered if this would be among his earliest memories—the rumble of the subway, the bike trip down Broadway behind the smoky bus, and the shirtless guy in a leather jacket shouting instructions and choosing protest signs like a fashion designer chooses blouses moments before the start of a runway show.

As the evening approached, Elliott and I turned back towards Brooklyn, and as we hit the foot of the Brooklyn Bridge, I noticed a sight that made me homesick (or at least home-away-from-homesick): a Dutch bike from Henry's shop, WorkCycles, leaned up against the concrete guard wall. In Amsterdam such a bike would be commonplace, but here in New York they tend to belong to either the fashion-conscious or members of the bike advocacy set. In this case it was the latter, and members of the advocacy group Transportation Alternatives were handing out bells to commuters on their way home from work.

I have a bell on my bike. I put it there during the last NYPD bike ticketing blitz, since they're technically required by law and I figured I shouldn't give them any excuses to write me a summons. (The truth is, it probably wouldn't have mattered, since people got tickets for stuff that wasn't even illegal, like not wearing a helmet or cycling outside of a bike lane—or, in a number of cases, swerving to avoid a police car parked in the middle of the bike lane.) I'm not even sure how useful a bell is in New York City, where the delightfully meditative "ding" is easily drowned out by loud car stereos and roaring elevated subways and Cadillac horns that play the theme from *The Godfather*, and indeed the only use I've found for it is that it amuses Elliot. I like to ring it before we set off on a ride: "Ding!" goes the bell, "Bell!" exclaims Elliott, and we set off into traffic where, in the event I need to alert someone to my presence, I forgo the bell in favor of a hearty "Look out, cocksucker!" (Elliott's going to learn that word sooner or later, so it might as well be in the context of safety.)

Nevertheless, it made me happy to see the Transportation Alternatives people handing out bells, and between the little ring-a-ding party and the idealistically unkempt Occupy protestors I couldn't help feeling a little bit of a tingling sensation in the place where I hide my heart. I started imagining a New York where it was once again possible to live in Manhattan if you weren't an investment banker, and where you might actually be able to ride a bike without getting run over by an investment banker. It was September but it still felt like summer, I was riding home to meet my wife who was now riding one of those Q trains over the neighboring bridge, and my son was behind me, happily chattering away.

Really, I had pretty much everything in life I could possibly want—except for feeling like a human being while riding a bike. I suppose in the grand scheme of things this was a minor problem, and I also suppose in a sense I was exactly like the Portlanders complaining about the streetcar tracks. Still, I couldn't help thinking how great the city could be if only it took after its Dutch parent a little more, and I started daring to think that maybe it could.

We're a funny country where cycling is concerned. We're home to some of the world's biggest bike companies, and we produce (or at least design) many of the world's most coveted bikes and accessories. In recent decades we've been at the forefront of the sport of professional cycling. We're the home of the hand-built custom bicycle renaissance, we invented mountain biking, we're driving the urban cycling trend, and there's probably not a city or town where a hardcore cyclist couldn't find a group ride.

Yet despite all of this, people don't think you belong on the road, and if you get killed by a driver while on your bike odds are nothing will happen to that driver.

I'm sure we'll continue to produce fancy bikes, and I'm sure the pastime of cycling will continue to grow, and I'm even reasonably sure they'll keep building bike lanes.

But as for losing our hatred and contempt for "weak stuff," I'm not always so sure.

INTERLUDE: STASIS

Sara, Elliott, and I spent the last week of 2011 in Montauk, the town that sits on the very tip of the south fork of Long Island. If you've never been there, it looks and feels like a hybrid of a New England fishing village and a surf town, because that's more or less what it is. Montauk is technically at least a hundred miles east of the New York City line, but practically speaking it's more like fifteen miles away, since that's where the area known as the Hamptons begins, and with its exclusive restaurants, high-end retail, and weekending financiers and celebrities, it's essentially a Manhattan annex. Montauk, however, despite also seeing its share of visitors from the city, still retains something of an air of seclusion.

This was our first real escape since the Europe trip, and we savored the relative tranquility. In an act of decadence, I brought two bicycles with me, and every morning I'd either ride my mountain bike on the trails of the nearby state park, or else I'd ride my road bike west past the dunes and into the Hamptons, and then east again all the way to the lighthouse that sits on Montauk Point. I've always savored the feeling of being on that point. Having spent my entire life on the very western end of Long Island, it feels good to be as far from home as possible while still remaining on the same sandbar. It's like leaving but not leaving. There's not a single bridge or tunnel between me and home, and the train tracks run in an unbroken line from Montauk all the way back to New York City, yet when I look out east past that lighthouse I know there's nothing else there until you hit Europe.

And so pretty much every morning I'd ride back and forth, west towards the city and then east to the very end of the island. West towards the little mini Manhattan, and east to the last stop on Long Island before you hit Europe. It was meditative. I just went back and forth, and as I did I thought about the past year's travels. I'd undertaken them wondering where I belonged, and I still didn't know.

chapter 13:

ON THE
ROAD
AGAIN

We'd just gotten back from Amsterdam when I received the following email:

Hallo

Sorry for my english,

I am a freelance journalist and currently working in the press office of a public body.

Our cultural association is located in Puglia in southern Italy and is involved in photography, video recordings etc, but also to promote the use of the bicycle. Four of us (males) are passionate about cycling, but we are amateurs. Females less . . . jokes aside we would be more than happy to accommodate your book to present the Bike Snob (which we all appreciate), and maybe make advances on the new one. The day of the May 12, 2012, called FULL DAY BIKE, will take place in this way: In the morning we will make a small trip walk of about 16 km from the town of San Vito dei Normanni and the Oasis of Torre Guaceto near the sea. A peaceful rally! Then we will make a social lunch. In the afternoon we will inaugurate a photo exhibition titled "Bike 24 shots" and at 18:00 will present your book and let you have a question. Then will project music video alternative music with images inside of bicycle and then . . . go to sleep. We offer hospitality in a luxury hotel in the countryside of Puglia (www.tenutamoreno.it) for 2 or 3 days and try to book airplane ticket for A / R . . .

do you like this?

p.s. I sending you a photo of the three organizers. I am in the middle with the black shirt . . .

too cool for you?

greetings Vincenzo

Despite the fact that Vincenzo was almost certainly using Google Translate to communicate with me, and even though I suspected that in southern Italy a "cultural association" might mean "Mafia," I informed Vincenzo that I did indeed, as he put it, "like this." I suppose this was mostly because I had just gotten back from Europe and missed it, and also because I had had such a good experience in Sweden when I answered a similar (though more articulate) invitation—though I'd be lying if I said I wasn't just a little bit intrigued by the luxury hotel's website, which included images of palm trees and hot tubbing. In any case, I accepted the invitation.

In the ensuing months I held out hope that Vincenzo's communications would become more intelligible, but this was not the case. Each communiqué would zigzag disorientingly between clarity and ambiguity, and just when a relatively comprehensible phrase like "I enclose the official poster of the 'Full Day Bike.' Like you?" (accompanied by said poster depicting a silhouetted mountain biker descending from the sky) lulled me into a false sense of security, I'd then be confronted with something totally nonsensical like "We feel when I get back from London!" So as the date for my visit to Italy drew closer, my understanding of just what it was I was supposed to be doing at "Full Bike Day" remained elusive.

Speaking of London, as my overseas travel plans came together, I made arrangements to visit it again on my way to Italy. The morning after my arrival I boarded a train to Birmingham and visited the Brooks saddle factory, a low brick building surrounded by the crumbling remains of Britain's industrial heyday and filled with hissing and pounding machinery that was a stunning contrast to Timothy Everest's dandified townhouse in gentrified Shoreditch. If Brooks had invited me there to brainwash me into believing in their company, then they succeeded, since few enterprises ooze character like a bunch of affable, hardworking British people happily making saddles as they have done for something like a century while the rest of the cycling industry shifts its manufacturing to Taiwan.

The next day, Jack Thurston (who had availed me of his apartment the last time I'd visited) led me on a ride from central London to the countryside in Kent—my first time riding a bicycle there outside of the city. As we made our way southeast, we passed through the double-decker chaos of the Elephant and Castle roundabout, and then through upscale boroughs bustling with comfortable-looking people dropping their comfortably tousled children off at school, then through the outer suburbs with their indistinguishable row houses—and then the city just abruptly fell away. Suddenly, we were on narrow, undulating roads surrounded by greenery and dotted with thatched-roof cottages and rambling pubs. There were footpaths and bridle paths and routes which Jack told me were once pilgrims' paths to Canterbury, and it really wasn't too hard to imagine what it must have looked like back then since besides the occasional Range Rover or Audi there was little indication that we were in the twenty-first century. The only reminders that we were still in the region of one of the world's largest, most important metropolises was the occasional wrong turn that would put us on a road with heavy car traffic, or when we would pass over the M25 motorway.

New York is part of a vast megalopolis interrupted only by natural borders. Where I live, city sprawls into city—Baltimore into Philadelphia into Newark into New York into Stamford into New Haven into Boston and so on—and any lush green countryside is mostly pockets of quasi-rural affluence. Kent may have been a giant pocket of quasi-rural affluence as well, but it also gave me the sense that for all its size and influence London was just a town like any other (albeit a giant town that had gobbled up many smaller towns), and like a town it knew its boundaries and had a clear end. It made me think of the zebra crossings. Maybe the fundamental difference between London and New York, or England and America, is this acceptance of containment and respect for boundaries. I suppose it's mostly a matter of scale. Kent is the "Garden of England." There's no "Garden of America." There are sprawling cities and mountains and wilderness and stretches of farmland that comprise entire states. I suppose the bigger your house, the less likely you are to be tidy.

Very early the next morning I left overcast London, and in the afternoon I landed in sunny Brindisi, Italy, where I was greeted by Vincenzo, his accomplice Andrea, and an interpreter by the name of Daniela. My first impression of the region was that it reminded me of Florida, since it was flat and hot and inhabited by people with tans, gold sunglasses, and snug clothing. Vincenzo ushered me into a van, in which he shuttled me to the fancy hotel with the hot tub for just long enough to ply me with sandwiches. Then it was back to the van for the various appointments Vincenzo had made for me. Between my profound jet lag and the fact that by necessity all communication had to run through Daniela, I felt vaguely like a very pampered hostage.

Our first appointment was at the newspaper *La Gazzetta del Mezzogiorno,* which was housed in a dingy office in Brindisi, where a man with a tan and boxy eyeglasses asked me (through Daniela) what I thought about doping in professional cycling and then another man with a tan and boxy eyeglasses took my picture. Then they took me on a long tour of the Torre Guaceto seaside nature preserve Vincenzo had mentioned in his email, and finally, as sleep deprivation was actually causing me to mistake olive trees for humans, to a bike shop in Vincenzo's town of San Vito dei Normanni.

The bike shop didn't have a name, and after three generations in business it seemed simply to operate as "the bike shop." Even though it was Friday evening and the sun was setting, people filled the tiny space and spilled out on the sidewalk, where an apprentice with a tan and boxy eyeglasses diagnosed shifting problems on racing bikes. I got the sense that at least half the people hanging around the shop didn't even own bikes and were simply there to watch, since men (there was not a woman in sight at the shop, apart from Daniela) tend to gravitate to any sort of work being performed on any sort of expensive vehicle.

In fact, I had no idea why Vincenzo had taken me here that perhaps he wanted to do the same—or, more profoundly, he wanted to watch me watch people work on fast racing bicycles. In any case, clearly very little had changed at this shop since the owner's grandfather had started it, apart from the fact that the Bottechias and Cinelles which he was assembling were made of carbon fiber in Taiwan instead of steel in Italy.

But while the sweatsuit–clad menfolk of San Vito dei Normanni were clearly enraptured by the sight of carbon racing bicycles costing many thousands of dollars, there was relatively little evidence in the area of cycling as a means of transportation, and the everyday riders I did see tended to be much older. You could easily imagine a time when many more people traveled the narrow streets of this medieval town by bicycle, and every so often I'd see a person riding, or a city bicycle leaned jauntily against the curb in front of a store, but for the most part it was clear that most of their grandchildren had moved on to cars and motorbikes.

The next morning I found that my picture had made *La Gazzetta del Mezzogiorno*. There I was, posing awkwardly with the Italian edition of my book, and clearly I had looked as disheveled as I had felt because my image evoked paparazzi shots of Whitney Houston in her final days. This only added to my feelings of insecurity, for ever since arriving in Italy I had been feeling acutely self-conscious. After all, this was the country of the Giro d'Italia, and the Fausto Coppi/Gino Bartali Rivalry, and of storied bicycle companies like Colnago and Pinarello. Sure, even though the Giro was going on during my visit nobody seemed to be paying attention to it, but nevertheless, Italy is to competitive cycling what Amsterdam is to bicycle commuting— the motherland, the great wellspring of cyclesport's spirit and passion, steeped in olive oil and insouciance. Meanwhile, I couldn't even speak the language, and for all my mockery of the sport of professional cycling I couldn't help but feel that my American lack of bike heritage was plain for all to see.

This was also why I was rather aghast when I learned that Vincenzo had arranged for me to address a high school assembly that morning. If appearing on a BBC radio show with Britain's aging cultural elite had seemed oddly unwarranted, speaking at a high school assembly felt grossly inappropriate. Who was I to talk to these kids about bicycling? I was a wiseass bike blogger from New York who knew nothing of their town, and had only been there for about twelve hours. Plus, the only element of cycling I could possibly imagine appealing to high school kids was the whole fixed-gear craze. And while cities like Milan had already embraced it wholeheartedly, from what I could tell fixed-gears had yet to make it to this part of Italy. I'd been mocking and ridiculing this subculture for years, but here I was wishing I could evoke it in a pathetic gambit to try to "get down" with the "youth." What was I supposed to talk about? I was furious at Vincenzo for the fact that he was about to throw me to these pubescent wolves, and I very nearly staged a day-long hot tub sit-in by way of protest.

Ultimately, I did go to the high school, though, and a headmaster who, in his lavender sweater, was vastly cooler than any headmaster had a right to be introduced me to a group of students (mostly girls) who had made a big circle of their chairs in the hall. I launched into some speech about how bicycles represented freedom, and that the so-called "freedom" of the automobile was actually a trap of licensing, loan payments, insurance policies, traffic jams, high fuel costs, and all the rest of it. I likened a bicycle to an electric guitar, and said that it could be a means of self-expression and freedom from authority. I lamely hoped that this promise of liberation would appeal to them in a "fuck authority" sort of way, and then I looked at Daniela, who translated it all for them. Afterwards, they dutifully asked me the sorts of questions you're supposed to ask so that the teacher knows you've been paying attention, and then one girl asked me if I had ridden my bicycle from New York, which made everybody laugh. Finally, the headmaster concluded my talk for me by explaining that riding bicycles was a great way to actually engage the world, unlike simply frittering away a bunch of time on the Internet. His lavender sweater radiated a soothing authority as he spoke, and I suspected that in recent years his life had probably become a futile crusade against the siren song of Italian Facebook. It was a sound message, but one I would have been hypocritical to try to put forth, since I effectively make my living by frittering away a bunch of time on the Internet for a bunch of other people who do the same.

Afterwards, when we were finished, the headmaster took us all out for espresso—because we were in Italy.

The next morning was Sunday (Italian kids go to school on Saturday) and the awkwardly-named Full Bike Day, and we gathered in the piazza in San Vito dei Normanni for the "small trip walk of about sixteen kilometers from the town of San Vito dei Normanni and the Oasis of Torre Guaceto near the sea." As I rolled around in the increasingly hot sun the square filled with older people on city bikes and younger people in Lycra and parents with young children and even a bunch of kids from the high school class I had addressed the day before. By departure time there were probably a couple of hundred people happily chatting away as the local business owners stood by and watched with bemusement, and soon we were off, being led by a van blasting extremely loud Euro disco as well as all manner of international hits. Children laughed and swerved, parents chatted, members of the local racing club flitted about and marshaled the group, and soon we were at the Torre Guaceto nature preserve, on which I was already an expert thanks to my tour of two days ago.

During the course of the ride, I thought about how exactly a year ago I had been in Gothenburg, Sweden, and now here I was on the heel of the boot of Italy, pretty much on the opposite end of the continent. In climate, geography, "bike culture," and just plain culture, these two places were profoundly different, but I had been brought to both by the bike, and in both places I had found people who were unabashedly happy to be out riding together on a beautiful day. They'd also welcomed me as graciously as it's possible to welcome someone, despite my linguistic ineptitude and general air of befuddlement.

Later that day, during the "presentation" portion of Full Bike Day in which we sat on a stage and people asked me questions, someone wondered how to turn San Vito dei Normanni into a bike-friendly community. To me, this town of twenty thousand people with its medieval streets, flat terrain, and fair weather seemed eminently rideable, but to them of course they felt like victims of the very same things I did in New York City—namely impatient drivers, recalcitrant government, and a lack of infrastructure. As he spoke (or rather as Daniela spoke, since she still had to translate everything), I thought about the ride earlier that day and of the tremendous spirit of goodwill that had characterized it. I also thought about how all over America we have Bike to Work Days, and Bike to Work Weeks, and charity rides, and other celebrations of the bicycle, and how invariably happy everybody is—after which comes the inevitable lamentation of "If only we could do this every day."

It occurred to me then as he spoke that there's absolutely no reason we can't do this every day. It's simply a matter of riding a bike without needing a pretense or a flyer or a follow car to change your flat or a municipality telling you, "This is the day when we appreciate you, now go out and ride." The desire is there, it's strong in every city and every country I've visited, and whether they take it for granted as they do in Amsterdam or they do bearded backflips of exuberance as they do in Portland, the need and the desire to ride bikes is universal.

"Every day," I explained to the concerned San Vitoan, "can be Full Bike Day."

And you don't even need to make any goofy posters.

Shortly after I returned to New York, Sara, Elliott, and I headed off on a ride in Brooklyn. It was a beautiful May weekend, and everywhere there were stoop sales—it was as though every brownstone in Park Slope had spat up its contents onto its front steps, and rather then put them back inside again the owners had simply said, "Oh, what the hell, let's just sell this stuff." People packed Prospect Park for some sort of artisanal food festival. Fifth Avenue was closed for a street fair. Cars could barely move. And everywhere, people seemed to be traveling by bike.

There were single people, couples, and families—kiddie seats and trailers and strange three-wheeled child-portaging contraptions I'd never seen and that must have cost near as much as a Hyundai.

It wasn't Amsterdam, and New York certainly will never be Amsterdam. But why would you want it to be? New York is New York. At the same time, there were more people and families simply riding bikes to get around than maybe I'd ever seen around here outside of an organized Full Bike Day–esque event. I wondered something:

were the traffic and the fair weather simply conspiring to force people onto their bikes for a day, or were we finally arriving as a true cycling city? After all, family cycling was the "final frontier," and here were people crossing that frontier in veritable wagon trains of smugness with nary a thought. Maybe we'd reached some sort of watershed moment.

Portland, New York, London, Amsterdam, Gothenburg, and San Vito dei Normanni have little in common, but in visiting them all under the auspices of the bicycle I'm left with a feeling of inevitability—that everywhere, people want to ride bikes. In some of these places they're looking around and wondering how they can do it, and if they can do it, and what they need in order to do it, but it's only a matter of time before they all turn to each other and realize that there's really nothing stopping them from riding.

A bike goes where you look, and riding one is a matter of both trusting the bike and forgetting about it. If we all stop looking at the bike and the clothes and all the rest of it and simply trust in the beauty of riding and look ahead, we're bound to get somewhere. And I think most of us are headed in the same direction.

ACKNOWLEDGMENTS

Thank you to Hans Stoops and the Komet Club Rouleur for bringing me to Gothenburg, to Henry Cutler for making our family feel so at home in Amsterdam and for giving us so much insight, to Jack Thurston for putting us up in London, and to Vincenzo De Leonardis for his sense of humor and for marching me around Brindisi (and special thanks to Daniela Giulia for interpreting). Thank you also to my editor Emily Haynes and my agent Danielle Svetcov for making this book possible, and to everyone at Chronicle for all their talent and hard work. And thanks New York City Department of Transportation for the bike lanes. Keep them coming!